ESCAPE OF THE DAMNED: RISING FROM DESPAIR, CONQUERING THE DARKNESS WITHIN AND BEYOND

VEDANT SINGH

BLUEROSE PUBLISHERS
India | U.K.

Copyright © Vedant Singh 2024

All rights reserved by author. No part of this publication may be reproduced, stored in a retrieval system or transmitted in any form or by any means, electronic, mechanical, photocopying, recording or otherwise, without the prior permission of the author. Although every precaution has been taken to verify the accuracy of the information contained herein, the publisher assume no responsibility for any errors or omissions. No liability is assumed for damages that may result from the use of information contained within.

BlueRose Publishers takes no responsibility for any damages, losses, or liabilities that may arise from the use or misuse of the information, products, or services provided in this publication.

For permissions requests or inquiries regarding this publication,
please contact:

BLUEROSE PUBLISHERS
www.BlueRoseONE.com
info@bluerosepublishers.com
+91 8882 898 898
+4407342408967

ISBN: 978-93-6783-454-1

First Edition: October 2024

How can this book be your starting point?

The Escape of the Damned

In the shadowed corridors of existence, where dreams flicker like candle flames against the relentless tide of despair, there lies a profound truth: every soul bears the weight of its own damned circumstances. Life, with its merciless twists and unyielding challenges, often binds us in chains of our own making. Yet within that darkness, an ember smoulders—an indomitable spirit yearning for release.

"The Escape of the Damned" serves not merely as a title, but as a clarion call to every warrior caught in the throes of despair, beckoning forth those who have felt the cold grip of defeat. It speaks to the silent struggles faced in the solitude of night, where one's inner demons dance with haunting clarity, whispering tales of inadequacy and despair. Each of us has felt the bitter sting of circumstance, the weight of expectations, and the suffocating embrace of societal norms that bind us. These bindings can feel like curses, damning us to a life of mediocrity and unfulfilled potential.

But herein lies the heart of our narrative—a journey not just of escape, but of transformation. To be "damned" is not to be irrevocably lost; rather, it is the starting point of an extraordinary odyssey. Within this book, you will uncover the wisdom and resilience hidden beneath layers of doubt and fear. The path to self-improvement is often shrouded in mist, and the journey is rarely linear, yet each step taken in defiance of despair leads to a profound awakening.

Imagine, if you will, a warrior awakening from a long slumber, wrapped in the remnants of battle-worn memories. This warrior, like many of us, has been defeated—not by external foes, but by the very circumstances of existence that sought to define them. Yet, it is in this moment of reckoning, where pain meets possibility, that the true magic of transformation begins. Each trial endured is but a forge, shaping resilience from the raw material of despair.

As you delve deeper into this tale, you will encounter the lessons etched into the fabric of life itself. You will meet others who have walked the same shadowy path, souls intertwined in a dance of fate, each sharing stories of struggle and redemption. From these encounters, you will glean insights that ignite the spark of change, encouraging you to rise as the warrior you were always meant to be.

The act of escaping one's damnation is both a solitary endeavour and a communal symphony. It is a dance of heartbeats, echoing in the chambers of shared experience, where vulnerability meets strength. In these pages, the whispers of countless souls resonate—each voice a reminder that we are never truly alone in our battles. Together, we form a constellation of hope, illuminating the path for those who dare to rise.

The journey of self-improvement requires courage; it demands a fierce commitment to confront the shadows that lurk within. Yet it is through this confrontation that we reclaim our power. "The Escape of the Damned" is not merely a story of flight, but an exploration of what it means to embrace our scars as badges of honour. Each wound tells a tale of survival, each setback a stepping stone toward the realisation of our true selves.

As you embark on this journey, let the title resonate within you. Embrace the idea that to be damned is not a permanent state but a transient phase—an invitation to unearth the warrior that lies dormant within. With every turn of the page, you will be guided to confront your own limitations, dismantle the narratives that have held you captive, and rise from the ashes of your own making.

In the end, the escape is not an act of fleeing, but an act of claiming. Claiming your narrative, your voice, and your destiny. The circumstances that have damned you do not define your worth; they are but chapters in a greater epic—an epic that you are destined to write. With every triumph and trial, you will carve out your place in the world, emerging not just as a survivor, but as a radiant warrior, emboldened by the fires of adversity.

So, dear reader, prepare yourself to venture into the unknown. As you navigate the realms of self-discovery, remember: you are not alone in your fight. The echoes of the damned are merely a whisper away, guiding you toward your escape. Embrace this journey, for it is within these pages that you will find the strength to rise, the courage to transform, and the wisdom to truly live.

Welcome to "The Escape of the Damned"—a testament to the power of the human spirit, a chronicle of rebirth, and a celebration of the relentless pursuit of self-improvement. As the story unfolds, may you find your own escape and emerge victorious, a warrior ready to embrace the life you were meant to lead.

Also understand, that I do not present a formula in this book but my story as a student, a person, an entrepreneur, a man and as a son. You might say well…. I don't have such problems…. We'll see down the road. Circumstances may differ, but the deeper patterns and lessons keep resonating.

As I have gotten more and more experienced through life, I have realised that just by making a few adjustments in our daily life like exercising only 30 minutes a day or making that call to your family and friends in that little 10 minutes break while in the office can make a hell of a difference. So with you all knowing about the vision of mine while being behind the keyboard, I wanted to share all that I have to, with you guys so that if anyone is struggling like I used to — I can be their outlet for something magnificent which we all will be proud of. Best wishes to you all as you proceed through these pages ……

Vedant Singh, Author

Chapter 1: Getting Ready

Jordan Peterson, in his book **Beyond Order,** says, in reference to his previous book **12 Rules For Life,** "*The message which I hoped to deliver was: When you are visited by chaos and swallowed up, when nature curses you or someone you love with illness; or when tyranny rends asunder something of value that you have built, it is salutary to know rest of the story. All of that misfortune is only the bitter half of the tale of existence, without taking note of the heroic element of redemption or the nobility of the human spirit requiring a certain responsibility to shoulder*".

Mr. Peterson, here elucidates why we shouldn't just focus on the negative aspect of the story but on the story as a whole. The story of you crafting your own pieces of life. Your decisions and the consequences they invite. You see to first know your bare chances of survival – to succeed that is – you are going to start somewhere. The first thing would be to become aware of the responsibilities that are adjoining your life right now. From the very basics like trying your best at studies and academics to paying the bills, all alongside making sure that your life doesn't suck. This, ladies and gentlemen, is the very basis of existence. The very basis of being acknowledged, of being respected. When you make sure that all your tasks align with your responsibilities, leading towards their completion and those responsibilities benefit you and the society, is when you start to experience a greater and heightened sense of righteousness.

Remember you have sources of strength upon which you can draw, and even though they may not work well, they may just be enough. You have what you can learn if you can accept your error. If you are not communicating about anything that engages other people, then the value of your communication - even the value of your very presence – risks falling to zero.

First, let's talk about Communication. People exist among other people and not as purely individual minds. People remain mentally healthy not merely because of the integrity of their own minds, but because they are constantly being reminded how to think, act and speak by those around them. If you begin to deviate from the path – or begin to act improperly – people will cajole and criticize you back into place. You definitely wouldn't like to be poked for speaking the wrong word in a social setting. So understand that Communication is the prerequisite for expression. Expressing yourself in the most liberal and most professional sense is all done by words. Let's understand it in detail.

Accepting Maximal Responsibility

Accepting maximal responsibility for growth is an essential tenet of personal development, intertwining individual agency with the broader tapestry of existence. This philosophy posits that individuals are not mere vessels subjected to external whims but rather architects of their own destinies. Embracing this profound responsibility catalyzes transformative change, fostering resilience, self-awareness, and a nuanced understanding of the intricate interplay between the self and the universe.

The Essence of Responsibility

At the heart of this discourse lies the concept of responsibility, a term often laden with connotations of obligation and duty. However, to grasp the full import of accepting responsibility for one's growth, we must delve deeper into its etymological roots. The word "responsibility" derives from the Latin *respondere*, meaning "to respond." Thus, true responsibility transcends passive acceptance; it embodies an active engagement with one's circumstances, a conscious decision to respond to life's vicissitudes with intention and purpose.

Agency and Empowerment

Maximal responsibility engenders a profound sense of agency. When individuals acknowledge their role in shaping their own growth, they reclaim their power. This empowerment is not merely about self-sufficiency but rather about cultivating a mindset that recognizes the potential for self-actualization. In the realm of psychology, this concept aligns with Carl Rogers' notion of the "fully functioning person," who embraces their experiences, learns from them, and integrates these lessons into their self-concept.

This agency manifests in myriad ways—through goal-setting, self-reflection, and the willingness to confront uncomfortable truths. By eschewing a victim mentality, individuals unlock the door to resilience. The challenges that once seemed insurmountable morph into opportunities for growth, inviting individuals to engage with discomfort rather than retreating from it. This paradigm shift fosters a proactive approach to life, encouraging exploration, experimentation, and, ultimately, evolution.

The Interconnectedness of Growth

One cannot discuss personal growth in isolation; it is inherently relational and communal. Accepting maximal responsibility involves recognizing the interconnectedness of our journeys with those of others. Each individual's growth is inextricably linked to the societal, cultural, and environmental contexts in which they reside. This awareness cultivates empathy, as one begins to appreciate the myriad influences that shape not only their own trajectory but also those of others.

Moreover, this interconnectedness imparts a sense of accountability that extends beyond the self. When individuals acknowledge their influence on the collective, they become stewards of their communities. This sense of responsibility cultivates a culture of support, where individuals uplift one another in their pursuits of growth. The ripple effect of one person's commitment to self-improvement can inspire others, creating a cascade of positive change.

Self-Awareness and Reflection

To accept maximal responsibility for one's growth necessitates a profound degree of self-awareness. This introspective journey is often fraught with challenges, as it demands an honest appraisal of one's strengths and weaknesses. The process of self-reflection, while uncomfortable, is indispensable for identifying areas in need of growth and development. Through practices such as journaling, mindfulness, and meditation, individuals can cultivate a deeper understanding of their thoughts, emotions, and behaviors.

This self-awareness serves as a compass, guiding individuals through the labyrinth of life. It enables them to recognize patterns in their decision-making and responses to challenges. When one understands the underlying motivations for their actions, they can make more informed choices that align with their authentic selves. This alignment is crucial for sustaining personal growth; it ensures that individuals are not merely reacting to external pressures but are instead pursuing paths that resonate with their core values and aspirations.

The Role of Adversity

Adversity, often perceived as a formidable foe, is, in fact, a crucible for growth. Accepting maximal responsibility entails embracing life's challenges as opportunities for learning and development. Resilience is cultivated in the face of hardship, and those who confront adversity head-on emerge with a fortified sense of self. This process is beautifully encapsulated in Friedrich Nietzsche's aphorism, "That which does not kill us makes us stronger."

When individuals accept responsibility for their growth amidst adversity, they cultivate a growth mindset, a term popularized by psychologist Carol Dweck. This mindset fosters the belief that abilities and intelligence can be developed through dedication and hard work. Rather than viewing setbacks as failures, individuals begin to see them as integral components of the learning process. This shift in perspective not only enhances resilience but also encourages a lifelong commitment to growth and self-improvement.

Cultivating a Growth-Oriented Environment

While personal responsibility is paramount, the environments we inhabit also play a significant role in shaping our growth. To fully embrace responsibility, individuals must curate spaces—both physical and emotional—that nurture their aspirations. This involves surrounding oneself with like-minded individuals who prioritize growth and self-improvement. The influence of a supportive community cannot be overstated; it serves as a catalyst for motivation and accountability.

Moreover, creating an environment conducive to growth entails seeking out resources—books, workshops, mentors—that challenge and inspire. In an age saturated with information, discernment is key. Individuals must take the initiative to filter the noise and focus on the inputs that align with their growth objectives. This proactive approach to learning reinforces the principle of responsibility, as individuals become active participants in their own education.

The Pursuit of Lifelong Learning

Maximal responsibility is inextricably linked to the pursuit of lifelong learning. Accepting responsibility for one's growth necessitates a commitment to continual exploration and curiosity. The world is replete with knowledge waiting to be discovered, and the journey of learning is both expansive and exhilarating. By embracing a learner's mindset, individuals open themselves to a wealth of experiences that enrich their lives and broaden their horizons.

In this context, failure takes on a new significance. Rather than being a deterrent, it becomes a vital component of the learning process. The most innovative thinkers and pioneers throughout history have embraced failure as a stepping stone to success. By accepting responsibility for their mistakes and using them as fodder for growth, individuals cultivate resilience and adaptability—qualities that are indispensable in an ever-evolving world.

The Symphony of Growth

In summation, accepting maximal responsibility for one's growth is a transformative journey that encompasses agency, interconnectedness, self-awareness, resilience, and a commitment to lifelong learning. It is a philosophical stance that empowers individuals to navigate the complexities of existence with intention and purpose. By embracing this responsibility, one not only enhances their own life but also contributes to the collective growth of humanity.

This journey is not linear; it is a symphony, a complex interplay of melodies that evolve and intertwine. Each note of challenge, each chord of triumph, contributes to a richer understanding of the self and the world. In this grand opus of personal development, accepting maximal responsibility is the refrain that echoes through the ages, urging us to become the architects of our destinies.

Part I:
Morality and Mortality

The Essence of Morality in the Pursuit of Success

Morality refers to the principles and standards that govern our behaviour, determining what is right or wrong. It provides a framework within which we make decisions and interact with others. In the pursuit of success, morality acts as a guiding compass, helping individuals navigate complex situations and maintain integrity. Success achieved without moral consideration can be fleeting and hollow, whereas success grounded in strong ethical values tends to be more fulfilling and enduring.

1. Ethical Foundations of Success

The concept of success often brings to mind the accumulation of wealth, power, or status. However, true success is deeply rooted in ethical behaviour. For instance, leaders like Nelson Mandela or Mahatma Gandhi are celebrated not only for their achievements but also for their moral fortitude. Their success was intertwined with their commitment to justice, equality, and the greater good. Their stories illustrate that success aligned with moral values often leads to a legacy that transcends mere personal gain.

2. Building Trust and Reputation

Morality is integral to building trust and credibility, which are essential for long-term success. In business, maintaining ethical standards fosters trust among clients, partners, and employees. Companies that prioritize ethical practices tend to enjoy better reputations and stronger relationships with stakeholders. For example, Patagonia, the outdoor clothing company, has garnered respect and loyalty by committing to environmental sustainability and ethical labour practices, demonstrating that moral principles can drive commercial success.

3. Navigating Ethical Dilemmas

The path to success is often fraught with ethical dilemmas. These are situations where competing values or interests challenge our moral compass. Navigating these dilemmas requires a steadfast commitment to ethical principles. For example, a manager might face the temptation to cut corners for short-term gain, but choosing to uphold ethical standards despite pressure demonstrates a commitment to long-term success and integrity.

Mortality:

The Awareness of Life's Finite Nature

Mortality, or the awareness of our finite existence, profoundly impacts our approach to success. Understanding that life is limited encourages individuals to make choices that reflect their values and aspirations. This awareness can serve as a catalyst for meaningful action and personal fulfilment.

1. **Motivation and Prioritization**

Recognizing our mortality can be a powerful motivator. It prompts us to reflect on what truly matters and prioritize our goals accordingly. For example, Steve Jobs, in his famous Stanford commencement address, spoke about how facing death helped him focus on what was truly important to him, leading to innovations that changed the world. The awareness of our limited time can drive us to pursue our passions more fervently and make decisions that align with our deepest values.

2. **Legacy and Impact**

The concept of legacy is deeply intertwined with mortality. Individuals often strive to leave a positive impact that outlasts their lifetime. This desire for a lasting legacy can drive people to achieve great things, but it also highlights the importance of moral considerations. A legacy built on ethical achievements and positive contributions to society tends to be more enduring and respected than one founded solely on personal gain. For instance, charitable philanthropists like Warren Buffet and Bill Gates focus on using their wealth to address global issues, ensuring that their success contributes to the greater good.

3. Facing Life's Impermanence

Mortality also teaches resilience and adaptability. The knowledge that life is transient encourages individuals to embrace challenges and view setbacks as opportunities for growth. This perspective can enhance the capacity to persevere through difficulties and maintain a focus on long-term goals. It helps cultivate a mindset that values effort and progress over mere outcomes, aligning success with a broader sense of purpose.

Integrating Morality and Mortality in the Pursuit of Success

Successfully integrating morality and mortality involves harmonizing ethical principles with an understanding of life's limited nature. This integration enriches the pursuit of success by ensuring that achievements are both personally satisfying and socially responsible.

1. Ethical Goal Setting

Setting goals with a moral dimension ensures that success is pursued in a manner that aligns with ethical standards. This involves defining success not only in terms of personal achievement but also in how it contributes to the well-being of others. For example, a social entrepreneur might set goals that address societal challenges, such as improving education or healthcare in underserved communities, thereby aligning personal success with a broader ethical mission.

2. **Purpose-Driven Success**

Success rooted in a sense of purpose is often more fulfilling. This purpose is shaped by an awareness of mortality and a commitment to moral values. Purpose-driven individuals are motivated by a vision that extends beyond personal gain, focusing on making a positive impact on the world. For instance, Malala Yousafzai's advocacy for girls' education is driven by both her personal values and a profound understanding of the importance of education in shaping a better future.

3. **Balancing Ambition and Ethics**

Balancing ambition with ethical considerations is crucial for sustainable success. Ambition can drive individuals to achieve extraordinary results, but it must be tempered with a commitment to ethical practices. This balance ensures that success is not achieved at the expense of others or through unethical means. For example, companies that adopt corporate social responsibility (CSR) initiatives demonstrate how ambition can be harmonized with ethical principles, contributing positively to society while pursuing business goals.

4. Reflection and Self-Awareness

Regular reflection on both our mortality and moral values enhances self-awareness and guides decision-making. This practice involves evaluating whether our actions align with our ethical beliefs and considering the impact of our decisions on our long-term legacy. Reflection fosters personal growth and ensures that success is pursued with integrity and purpose.

The interconnection between morality and mortality provides a profound framework for understanding and achieving success. Morality serves as a compass, guiding ethical behaviour and decision-making, while mortality reminds us of the finite nature of life, motivating us to pursue meaningful and impactful goals. By integrating these concepts, individuals can achieve success that is not only personally fulfilling but also aligned with a greater purpose and positive societal impact.

True success transcends mere material achievement, encompassing a holistic approach that values integrity, purpose, and contribution to the greater good. By aligning our actions with moral principles and recognizing the significance of our finite existence, we can navigate the path to success in a way that is both meaningful and enduring. This integrated perspective ensures that our pursuit of success enriches not only our own lives but also the lives of others, leaving a legacy that reflects our deepest values and aspirations.

An immoral man cannot withstand the pressure of life which blesses us with so many unenjoyable turns. It's simply because if you don't have your morals or set of rules to abide by, life just becomes a daily - go - through - drag which you have to go through again and again and every day.

At times like this, if you don't have words which inspire you to embrace the situation and take action - words which you think are the ones which can have a significant impact on you to get out of this situation, then honestly you are fucked. **Those wise words**. It doesn't matter if the words are from a philosopher which you encountered in a book or a few words from the "I trust you" speech your parents gave you. Keep plugging away and doing your best. Not only living with a set of rules or philosophy helps you to face dark situations but also it helps us to make better decisions by helping us to think more rationally which in turn allows oneself to become virtuous. There is a story I'd like to share when it comes to talking about being virtuous.

Long ago in Greece, Hercules was at crossroads. Where was he going? Or where was he trying to go? All to say, Hercules like so many of us did not know. As he progressed and the road diverged, Hercules was made a call by two goddesses who stood at the end of each path. On the first one there was a beautiful goddess who called out to him strongly. She said that she was willing to offer him every temptation he could ever imagine. Covered in finery, she promised him a life of ease. Follow her, she said, and his every desire would be fulfilled.

On the other path, stood a sterner goddess with a white robe who made a quieter call. She promised no rewards except those which came to him as a result of hard work. She said that it would be a long journey accompanied by scary experiences and sacrifices would have to be made but only a god could complete it.

Which path do you think Hercules chose? Doesn't it remind you of something that relates to most of us? Well, Hercules chose the second path. He chose virtue over vice. Doesn't this story remind you of the dilemma which we face today? Listen up. Every day we make choices. It may be about anything. Let's say you have got Math assignment to do. Now you can either ask your "true math genius" friend to complete it for you which you believe he is going to do to cope with his "improving his math skills" bullshit and regret at the time of examination for not studying at the correct time or you can just complete it by yourself and ask only for assistance if needed. This will be more time-consuming but will be worth it in the end.

The point here is if you know the good and bad of things and still are calling your "friend" to do it then most likely you are driven by short-term pleasure of freedom.

Also, I think that morality and mortality and interlinked or directly proportional so to speak. Let me elucidate how. If you are accustomed with good moral characteristics and raised up with certain values, you grow up in accordance to that. There are encounters along the way with people who you probably want to become like someday by understanding their ideologies and belief systems. If you actually work to that extent and make it to the point where you want to be in life – a millionaire for example – and use your morals for the good of the systems, you are immortal in a sense. Like if you use your, let's say, lump sum amounts of money to help other people and the environment and make use of some of your time to do things which other people can benefit off as well, you, on your deathbed, will leave behind some impact on people and will be remembered. Therefore, in a philosophical sense, you are never dead hence **immortal.** Sounds insane, I know but this is what my understanding of the world permits me to perceive.

The world as we know it today is not such a bad place if you know how to do good for the right kind of people. All you need is a heart and character. Today's world is full of uselessness. Young people, mostly, not all, are occupied by distractions and things which do not even matter instead of looking for opportunities to make their lives better along with millions of others. This – in my perception – is a thing to be done by cowards as they are afraid of competition.

As a consequence of the growing population, people who are noticing that their efforts are not getting compounded or are not enough – yet – give in and procrastinate, thereby delaying the end goal even more. The importance of the word "yet" cannot be elucidated. People today want instant gratification and hence they want what they like immediately, which simply isn't possible. Great things take time.

Coming back to our topic of Communication skills, the best way to develop them is mostly through putting yourself out there. The more you interact with people, the more you will learn. This is called **The Exposure Effect**. We will discuss it shortly.

Part II:
Mastering the Uncertain

For the longest time, I have questioned the functionality and significance of rules and codes of conduct. Is it necessary to conform, to be disciplined and to follow the rules? I always wondered. As I have grown up, I have had the answer. Yes. It is. But it is also necessary to use Judgement, Vision and the truth that guides conscience to tell what is right, when the rules suggest otherwise. It is the ability to manage this combination that truly characterizes the completely developed personality: A True Hero.

The hero could be you. How? Well start by acknowledging that there are fixable flaws. The uncertain begins from within. Light can only exist when there is darkness. So first delve into the darkness of your own bodily sanctum and try to commiserate with the darkness in you. Remember, Darkness signifies Evil. Bad Habits, ignorance of knowledge, ignorance of responsibilities and evil vices such as wishing bad for others....all fall in Darkness.

Not a long time ago, I contemplated on my own darknesses, out of which came my light. When I reflected on the necessary, I did so with the help of a Journal. Always. So I am just going to lay down what I wrote back in the day which gave me an idea on how to defeat my demons. This, Of Course, wasn't something I planned to publish but here I am. The time when I did reflect, was harsh. Hence I turned to my journal and started scribbling. To my utter surprise, my sentences started to make sense. Out of which came a conclusion. Truly, God's plans are better. I have arranged it in a more organised manner so that you guys could get the points. Also I have provided a list of questions at the end to let you do your own assessment since there's no one size fits all philosophy applicable here. Well, here you go..

In the labyrinth of existence, where uncertainties waltz with destiny and shadows dance with light, lies the enigmatic art of mastering oneself. To venture into the world and carve a niche of significance, one must first embark upon an inner odyssey—an exploration of the self that transcends the superficial and delves into the very essence of our being. This journey is not merely about honing skills or accumulating accolades but about unlocking the hidden recesses of one's soul, transforming from within, and emerging as a luminary in the vast expanse of the world.

The Enigma of the Self

To master the self is to engage in a sublime alchemical process, where the base elements of one's personality are transmuted into the gold of true mastery. This quest begins in the shadowy depths of introspection, where the self is laid bare, and the veil of pretence is lifted. In these uncharted realms, one encounters the raw, unpolished facets of their being—fears, desires, insecurities, and latent potentials.

1. The Abyss of Self-Reflection

Enter the abyss of self-reflection, where the mirror does not merely reflect but reveals. Here, the true self, stripped of societal masks and egoic adornments, is laid bare. This is not a realm for the faint-hearted. It is a domain where one must confront the shadows, the hidden aspects of the psyche that have long remained cloaked in darkness. It is through this confrontation that true self-awareness emerges, a potent force that lays the groundwork for mastery.

To dwell in this abyss is to engage in a dance with one's own inner demons, to listen to the echoes of the past, and to decipher the cryptic messages of one's deepest fears and desires. This process of self-unveiling is akin to unearthing buried treasure, where each revelation brings one closer to the core of their being.

2. The Paradox of the Inner Sanctum

Within this sanctuary of the self, paradoxes abound. Strength and vulnerability, confidence and doubt, clarity and confusion—these seemingly contradictory elements coalesce into a complex tapestry of existence. To master oneself, one must embrace this paradoxical nature, recognizing that the path to true mastery is not linear but a labyrinthine journey of integrating these dualities.

Here lies the alchemical secret: the true mastery of the self is achieved not by eradicating these paradoxes but by harmonizing them. It is in this delicate balance that one finds the key to unlocking their full potential, for it is only when the inner sanctum is understood and accepted in its entirety that external mastery becomes attainable.

Transmuting the Inner Essence into External Mastery

With the self-mastered and the inner sanctum illuminated, the journey progresses from the realms of introspection to the tangible world. The metamorphosis from an inwardly attuned being to an external force of significance involves the transmutation of one's essence into skill and action. This stage requires a delicate interplay between the self's newfound clarity and the external skills necessary to manifest one's place in the world.

1. The Crucible of Skill Crafting

In the crucible of skill crafting, raw potential is forged into expertise. This is where the alchemical principles *of transformation take centre stage. Each skill, whether it be the art of persuasion, the precision of craftsmanship, or the strategic acumen of leadership, begins as a mere fragment of possibility. Through relentless practice and a deep-seated commitment, these fragments are honed into refined, potent abilities.*

To engage in this process is to step into the forge of one's own creation. It is a journey marked by trials and tribulations, where each challenge serves as a catalyst for refinement. This stage is less about the destination and more about the journey of transformation. It requires patience, resilience, and an unwavering dedication to the craft.

2. The Convergence of Purpose and Skill

As skills are cultivated, they must converge with purpose. Purpose acts as the guiding constellation, directing the newly forged abilities toward meaningful ends. This convergence is not a mere alignment but a profound synthesis, where one's essence, shaped by self-mastery, melds with their skills to create a force of unique significance.

The alignment of purpose and skill is akin to the creation of a masterwork of art. It involves a nuanced understanding of one's role in the world and the impact that their skills can have. This synthesis transforms mere proficiency into mastery, where actions are imbued with intention, and skills are wielded with purpose.

3. The Art of Emergence

With the self mastered and skills refined, the final stage is the art of emergence. This is the moment when one steps into the world, not as a mere participant but as a sovereign entity of significance. It is a moment of revelation, where the internal mastery and external skills converge to create a presence that commands attention and respect.

The art of emergence involves navigating the world with a unique blend of confidence and humility, authority and empathy. It is the ability to stand firmly in one's truth while engaging with the world in a manner that resonates with authenticity and impact. This emergence is not a singular event but an ongoing process of adaptation and evolution, where one continuously refines their presence and contributions.

4. The Dance of the Mastery

At the heart of mastering oneself and the world lies a dance—a perpetual interplay between the internal and external realms. This dance is characterized by a fluid integration of self-awareness, skill refinement, and purposeful action. It is a dynamic process that requires continuous engagement, adaptation, and growth.

To partake in this dance is to embrace the rhythm of life, where mastery is not a static achievement but a living, evolving art. It involves attuning oneself to the ever-changing cadence of existence, responding with agility and grace to the challenges and opportunities that arise. This dance is a reflection of the harmonious balance achieved within, now expressed in the external world.

The Mystique of the Journey

In this enigmatic journey of mastering oneself and the world, the path is as significant as the destination. The process of self-discovery and skill development is imbued with mystery and wonder, where each step reveals new facets of potential and possibility. It is a journey marked by revelations, transformations, and the continuous quest for deeper understanding.

This journey is not for the faint of heart. It demands courage, perseverance, and an openness to the unknown. It invites one to embrace the mystery of their own existence, to venture into the shadows of their psyche, and to emerge with a profound sense of purpose and mastery. It is in this journey that true significance is found—not in the accolades or external markers of success, but in the profound alignment of self, skill, and purpose.

To master the uncertain is to embrace the mystique of existence, to navigate the labyrinth of self and skill with an open heart and a resilient spirit. It is a journey of becoming—a transformation from within that manifests as a powerful presence in the world. As one traverses this path, they become not merely participants in life but sovereign architects of their destiny, leaving an indelible mark on the tapestry of existence.

In this exploration of the self and the world, the mysteries unfold, revealing the profound truth that true mastery lies not in conquering the external but in unlocking the boundless potential within. It is a journey of alchemical transformation, where the core of one's being is illuminated, refined, and expressed in the grand symphony of existence.

Questions to reflect on :

1. What are the core values that define who I am, and how do they influence my actions and decisions?

2. In what ways have I encountered and confronted my inner fears and insecurities? How have these encounters shaped my self-awareness?

3. What are the paradoxes within myself that I struggle with, and how can I begin to harmonize these dualities to achieve personal growth?

4. What personal experiences or moments of introspection have revealed the most about my true self? How have these revelations impacted my sense of purpose?

5. Which skills do I currently possess that align with my inner values and purpose, and which areas require further refinement or development?

6. How do I currently use my skills in my daily life or career, and in what ways could these skills be enhanced to better align with my long-term goals?

7. What is my overarching purpose or mission in life, and how do I envision my skills contributing to this purpose?

8. How can I balance the pursuit of skill mastery with the need for authenticity and self-expression?

9. What are the external challenges or opportunities that I face, and how can my refined skills and self-awareness help me navigate them effectively?

10. In what ways can I continuously adapt and evolve my skills and self-awareness to maintain relevance and significance in a changing world?

I assume that you have read through this one hell of an art. It was only after reading the end product myself that I realised, I wanted to write. Hence began my journey of Poetry. Yes, I do write poetry. Quite often actually. But that's a story for another day. Now that you have the answers to your questions, its time to go further in the quest.

Once you have a skill or skills. Plural. You would need to hone it. You don't know when the path you are walking on may unfold unpleasantly. Better to be prepared. Now, since you know yourself, better, even though not completely (because if you would be knowing yourself to the utmost you wouldn't read the book), I believe the darkness within, has dimmed and the light has begun to shine brighter. How do you hone your skills though? Repetition. Understand that it takes time to build something. From LEGOs to a Career. So don't rush and take your time.

So now you have skills and know yourself better, the next step would be to go out into the world and get paid for them. Seems daunting, doesn't it? You'll get over it. With time. Your best bet would be to utilize resources which allow you to make a living remotely. You can use Websites like Freelancer.com or Upwork to get access to them.

But completely get one thing in that thinking box of yours that YOU AREN'T GOING TO GET A CLIENT RIGHT AWAY! It will take a considerable amount of time for you to sign your first clients. Simply because you are new to the platform and not many people know you. We will be discussing how to make money and being at the top in terms of finance later in the book.

To achieve greatness, it is essential to address and transcend one's own inner struggles while also cultivating the ability to perceive and nurture the potential goodness in others. Embracing this perspective allows one to identify and leverage opportunities for advancement, turning challenges into pathways for progress. By balancing self-improvement with an appreciation for the potential in those around us, we create a harmonious environment conducive to collective success. This dual approach not only fosters personal development but also encourages a collaborative spirit, ultimately leading to a more profound and impactful journey towards becoming the very best.

Thus, it is your perception and mindset that shape and define your place in the world. The way you view yourself and your surroundings determines the opportunities you encounter and the paths you choose. A positive and open mindset can transform challenges into stepping stones, while a limiting perspective may confine you to less fulfilling experiences. By cultivating a mindset that embraces growth and possibilities, you influence not only your own trajectory but also how you interact with and impact the world around you. Ultimately, your inner outlook plays a crucial role in determining your journey and your place within it.

Let us turn our attention to the most formidable and potent tool at your disposal: your mind. This extraordinary faculty, with its boundless capacity for thought, creativity, and insight, stands as the ultimate instrument for achieving greatness. To harness its full potential, one must engage in deliberate cultivation and refinement. By honing your cognitive abilities, expanding your intellectual horizons, and fostering a mindset of continuous growth, you empower yourself to navigate and influence the world with unparalleled efficacy.

Part III :

Orchestrating Your Mental Evolution and Building Fortitude

The mind, when meticulously developed, becomes a powerful engine of transformation and innovation, capable of transcending limitations and forging new pathways. Thus, the pursuit of intellectual and personal enrichment is not merely an endeavour but a profound journey towards mastering the art of self-actualization. Embracing this process with diligence and passion will enable you to unlock the vast reserves of potential within you and wield your mental faculties with precision and prowess. In doing so, you position yourself to make a significant and enduring impact on both your own life and the broader world.

Let us first understand what mental evolution means.

Mental evolution is a multifaceted concept that encapsulates the continuous process of enhancing cognitive abilities, emotional intelligence, and overall personal growth. At its core, mental evolution represents the dynamic journey of transforming one's mental faculties and emotional capacities to achieve greater self-awareness, intellectual agility, and emotional resilience.

1. **Cognitive Abilities**: Cognitive abilities refer to the mental processes that involve acquiring knowledge, understanding, reasoning, and problem-solving. Mental evolution in this context includes the development of skills such as critical thinking, analytical reasoning, and creativity. This evolution enables individuals to approach complex problems with innovative solutions, make informed decisions, and adapt to new information or changing circumstances.

2. **Emotional Intelligence**: Emotional intelligence (EI) encompasses the ability to recognize, understand, and manage one's own emotions, as well as the emotions of others. It involves skills such as empathy, emotional regulation, and effective communication. Enhancing emotional intelligence through mental evolution fosters healthier relationships, improved interpersonal interactions, and greater self-regulation, which are essential for both personal well-being and professional success.

3. **Personal Growth**: Personal growth refers to the ongoing process of self-improvement and self-discovery. This includes expanding one's

horizons, developing new skills, and cultivating a deeper understanding of oneself. Mental evolution supports personal growth by encouraging continuous learning, self-reflection, and the pursuit of meaningful goals, ultimately leading to a more fulfilling and purpose-driven life.

After knowing all of this, you might have a question on the importance of Mental Evolution, let's clear it out..

The Importance of Mental Evolution in Achieving Personal and Professional Goals

Mental evolution plays a critical role in achieving both personal and professional goals. It is not merely about enhancing individual capabilities but also about leveraging these advancements to create a positive impact on one's life and the lives of others. It helps improving problem – solving abilities, helps to improve one's Emotional Regulation, helps to build Resilience, helps with being more aware of oneself and helps with Fulfillment and Purpose. Now I understand that these are bold claims. Here's a bit more insight on each.

Enhanced Problem-Solving and Innovation: As cognitive abilities evolve, individuals develop the capacity to approach problems with greater creativity and innovation. Enhanced problem-solving skills enable individuals to navigate complex challenges more effectively and generate novel solutions. In a professional context, this leads to increased productivity, improved decision-making, and a competitive edge in dynamic and evolving industries.

1. **Improved Emotional Regulation and Resilience**: Developing emotional intelligence through mental evolution contributes to better emotional regulation and resilience. This means being able to manage stress, adapt to adversity, and maintain a balanced perspective in the face of challenges. For personal growth, this results in improved mental health and well-being. Professionally, it translates to enhanced leadership capabilities, effective teamwork, and the ability to handle high-pressure situations with composure.

2. **Greater Self-Awareness and Self-Management**: Mental evolution fosters greater self-awareness, allowing individuals to understand their strengths, weaknesses, and underlying motivations. This self-awareness is crucial for setting realistic and meaningful goals, both personally and professionally. It also supports effective self-management, enabling individuals to align their actions with their values and objectives, thereby achieving greater satisfaction and success.

3. **Enhanced Communication and Interpersonal Relationships**: Emotional intelligence is a key component of effective communication and building strong relationships. By evolving mentally, individuals improve their ability to empathize, listen actively, and communicate thoughtfully. In personal relationships, this results in deeper connections and more fulfilling interactions. Professionally, it leads to improved collaboration, conflict resolution, and leadership effectiveness.

4. **Increased Adaptability and Lifelong Learning**: Mental evolution instils a mindset of adaptability and a commitment to lifelong learning. This is particularly important in an era of rapid change and technological advancement. Individuals who embrace mental evolution are better equipped to stay relevant in their fields, adapt to new challenges, and continuously expand their knowledge and skills. This adaptability enhances career prospects and personal growth by ensuring that individuals remain agile and forward-thinking.

5. **Achievement of Personal Fulfillment and Purpose**: Personal growth achieved through mental evolution contributes to a deeper sense of fulfilment and purpose. By aligning personal goals with intrinsic values and passions, individuals can

experience a greater sense of meaning and satisfaction in their lives. This alignment also fosters a sense of achievement and contentment, enhancing overall well-being and quality of life.

6. **Professional Advancement and Success**: In the professional realm, mental evolution translates into career advancement and success. Enhanced cognitive abilities, emotional intelligence, and self-management skills contribute to better job performance, leadership potential, and career progression. Professionals who invest in their mental evolution are more likely to achieve their career goals, gain recognition, and make significant contributions to their organizations.

Practical Strategies for Mental Evolution

To facilitate mental evolution, individuals can engage in various practices and strategies that promote cognitive, emotional, and personal development:

1. **Continuous Learning**: Embrace opportunities for lifelong learning, whether through formal education, self-study, or experiential. learning. Engage with new ideas, challenge existing knowledge, and seek out diverse perspectives to stimulate intellectual growth.

2. **Mindfulness and Reflection**: Practice mindfulness techniques, such as meditation and journaling, to enhance self-awareness and

emotional regulation. Regular reflection helps individuals gain insights into their thoughts, emotions, and behaviours, fostering personal growth and development.

3. **Emotional Intelligence Training**: Develop emotional intelligence through Mantra Meditation and self-help resources. Focus on building skills such as empathy, active listening, and spiritual views to improve interpersonal relationships and self-management.

4. **Goal Setting and Action Planning**: Set clear, achievable goals and create action plans to track progress. Regularly review and adjust goals to ensure they align with evolving personal and professional aspirations. This structured approach supports continuous growth and achievement.

5. **Seek Feedback and Mentorship**: Solicit feedback from others and seek mentorship to gain valuable insights and guidance. Constructive feedback helps individuals identify areas for improvement and refine their skills, while mentorship provides support and encouragement for personal and professional development.

6. **Embrace Challenges and Step Out of Comfort Zones**: Actively seek out challenges and opportunities that push you beyond your comfort zone. Embracing new experiences and overcoming obstacles fosters growth, resilience, and adaptability.

7. **Foster Positive Relationships and Networks**: Build and nurture relationships with individuals who inspire, support, and challenge you. Surrounding yourself with positive influences and a supportive network contributes to personal growth and professional success.

You may already be familiar with many of these tips, but if you were not, you are now. Embracing these strategies will enhance your understanding and foster personal and professional growth, guiding you toward greater success and fulfilment.

Despite possessing this knowledge, our ability to implement these strategies effectively remains constrained. Engaging in these practices repeatedly, particularly when they are not yet second nature, can evoke vastly different responses. For some, this process may unfold as a profound and exhilarating experience, seamlessly integrating into their daily routine with enthusiasm and ease. In such cases, the pursuit of these practices feels rewarding and enriching, presenting no significant challenges.

Conversely, for those unaccustomed to these habits, the experience can be markedly less gratifying. The repeated effort may seem laborious and burdensome, as the initial resistance and discomfort can overshadow the potential benefits. Adapting to new practices requires a considerable investment of time and energy, and the transition from inertia to engagement can be fraught with difficulties. This disparity in experience underscores the inherent challenge of sustained commitment to self-improvement and personal development. It highlights the necessity of cultivating perseverance and resilience, even when the journey feels arduous. Ultimately, navigating this dichotomy demands both patience and determination, as the rewards of personal evolution often lie on the other side of initial discomfort and resistance.

In this context, resilience becomes paramount. To build resilience as formidable as a Viking's, it is essential to adopt scientifically-backed strategies that enhance mental and emotional fortitude.

Cognitive reframing is a crucial technique for developing resilience. This process involves shifting your perspective on challenges, viewing them not as insurmountable obstacles but as opportunities for growth. By changing the way you interpret stressors and setbacks, you reduce their negative impact on your mental well-being. Practising cognitive reframing helps to foster a more positive and adaptive mindset. **Emotional regulation** skills are also vital. Techniques such as mindfulness meditation and deep-breathing exercises can significantly improve your ability to manage and modulate emotional responses. Mindfulness encourages present-moment awareness and acceptance, reducing anxiety and stress. By learning to regulate your emotions effectively, you enhance your capacity to remain calm and composed under pressure. **Problem-solving abilities** further bolster resilience. Strengthening your problem-solving skills involves breaking down complex challenges into smaller, manageable tasks and employing strategic planning. This approach not only improves your ability to tackle obstacles but also enhances your adaptability and resourcefulness in navigating adversity. A strong **support network** plays a crucial role in building resilience. Surround yourself with supportive friends, family, and colleagues who provide emotional reinforcement and practical assistance during stressful times. Social support is a key factor in mitigating stress and enhancing overall resilience. **Regular physical exercise** contributes significantly to resilience by improving mood and stress resilience through the release of endorphins. Incorporating consistent physical activity into your routine supports both physical health and emotional stability. Cultivating a **growth mindset** is essential for long-term resilience. Embrace a mindset focused on continuous learning and self-improvement, viewing failures as learning opportunities rather than setbacks. This perspective encourages persistence and adaptability. Lastly, prioritizing **self-care** ensures that you maintain overall well-being. Adequate rest, proper nutrition, and relaxation are fundamental to sustaining mental and emotional resilience, enabling you to recover more effectively from stress.

By integrating these evidence-based strategies, you can fortify your resilience and approach life's challenges with the strength and fortitude of a Viking. (Not to mention me giving examples of a Viking because I absolutely LOVE them.)

Learning from books is undoubtedly, the greatest way to build up your mental fortitude. In the vast, enigmatic labyrinth of intellectual fortitude, few paths are as richly adorned with transformative potential as the journey through the boundless realms of literature.

You see, the ancient art of learning from books—those repositories of arcane knowledge and timeless wisdom—stands as an unparalleled method for fortifying the mind. Delving into the depths of these literary sanctuaries not only uncovers the hidden treasures of human understanding but also endows the seeker with a formidable mental resilience that defies the ordinary constraints of cognition.

Books, in their most profound essence, serve as vessels of profound knowledge, embedding within their pages the distilled essence of human experience and empirical discovery. Their pages, laden with the accumulated wisdom of centuries, offer more than mere narratives; they present an intricate tapestry of ideas and insights that challenge and expand the boundaries of the human intellect. Engaging with such texts catalyses a metamorphosis, akin to the alchemical transmutation of base elements into gold, nurturing the mental fortitude necessary to navigate the vicissitudes of existence. Mindset by Dr. Carol S. Dweck was a really good read for me. The concepts and ideas she presented were something which I adore till now and probably will continue to do so for my entire life and what better time to reveal my learnings from the book than now?

In *Mindset: The New Psychology of Success*, Carol Dweck introduces the transformative concept of the growth mindset, a belief that abilities and intelligence can be developed through dedication and hard work. This mindset contrasts sharply with the fixed mindset, which views traits and skills as static and unchangeable. Cultivating a growth mindset is not just about altering one's perspective but actively engaging in practices and adopting strategies that reinforce the belief in one's potential for growth. Through embracing challenges, learning from criticism, and valuing effort, among other approaches, individuals can foster a mindset that propels them towards greater achievement and personal development.

Embracing Challenges

One of the fundamental principles of a growth mindset is the embrace of challenges. Carol Dweck illustrates how individuals with a growth mindset view challenges not as obstacles but as opportunities for growth. For instance, students who struggle with a complex math problem are encouraged to persist, seeing each difficulty as a chance to deepen their understanding rather than a sign of inadequacy. This perspective is rooted in the belief that effort leads to improvement and that facing challenges is an integral part of the learning process. By shifting the focus from avoiding difficulties to tackling them head-on, individuals with a growth mindset are more likely to engage in the rigorous practice necessary for development.

Learning from Criticism

Another crucial element of a growth mindset is the ability to learn from criticism. Dweck contrasts the reaction to feedback between those with a growth mindset and those with a fixed mindset. The latter often view criticism as a personal affront, whereas those with a growth mindset perceive it as a valuable resource for improvement. For example, a manager who receives constructive feedback from colleagues might use it as a basis for making meaningful changes in their approach. By valuing feedback and viewing it as an opportunity for learning, individuals can continuously refine their skills and enhance their performance. This approach not only fosters personal growth but also promotes a culture of open communication and ongoing development.

Celebrating Effort, Not Just Results

Dweck emphasizes the importance of celebrating effort rather than merely acknowledging results. This shift in focus from innate ability to effort helps to reinforce the growth mindset. For instance, when children are praised for their perseverance and hard work rather than their intelligence, they come to understand that success is a result of effort and not just inherent talent. This recognition of effort encourages them to tackle new challenges and persist through difficulties. Celebrating effort aligns with the growth mindset's core belief that abilities can be developed through dedication, thereby motivating individuals to strive for continuous improvement.

The Power of "Yet"

One of the simplest yet most profound ways to cultivate a growth mindset is through the use of the word "yet." Dweck advocates for incorporating this term into self-talk to underscore the potential for growth. For example, if a student struggles with a particular concept, instead of feeling defeated, they might say, "I haven't mastered this yet, but I am working on it." This linguistic adjustment reframes the situation from one of failure to one of ongoing development. By adding "yet" to their self-assessment, individuals reinforce the idea that they are on a journey of growth and that current struggles are temporary obstacles rather than permanent limitations.

Viewing Failures as Learning Opportunities

Dweck's book also highlights the importance of viewing failures as opportunities for learning rather than as reflections of one's abilities. Through anecdotes of well-known figures such as Michael Jordan and Thomas Edison, who faced significant setbacks but ultimately achieved great success, Dweck illustrates how resilience and a positive attitude towards failure can lead to eventual triumph. For instance, Thomas Edison's numerous failed experiments before inventing the light bulb exemplify how persistent effort in the face of failure can lead to breakthrough innovations. Embracing failure as a learning experience rather than a defeat helps individuals to develop resilience and a mindset that values perseverance and growth.

Setting Learning Goals

Setting goals that focus on learning rather than mere performance is another effective strategy for nurturing a growth mindset. Dweck suggests that individuals should prioritize goals that emphasize the acquisition of new skills and understanding. For example, instead of setting a goal to achieve a specific grade on a test, a student might set a goal to fully comprehend a challenging concept or master a new technique. This shift from performance-oriented goals to learning-oriented goals encourages a focus on the process of development and the acquisition of knowledge. By valuing the journey of learning itself, individuals can cultivate a growth mindset that prioritizes continuous improvement and intellectual curiosity.

Transforming Self-Talk

The way individuals talk to themselves can significantly impact their mindset. Dweck advises transforming self-talk to reflect a growth mindset by emphasizing effort and potential rather than fixed abilities. For example, rather than thinking, "I am not good at this," individuals can adopt a more constructive self-talk approach, such as, "I am not good at this yet, but I can improve with practice." This change in self-talk helps to reinforce the belief that abilities can be developed over time and that current limitations are not permanent. By consistently using growth-oriented language, individuals can foster a mindset that embraces challenges and views setbacks as opportunities for growth.

Modelling a Growth Mindset

Finally, Dweck underscores the importance of modelling a growth mindset, particularly for leaders and educators. When leaders, parents, or teachers openly demonstrate their own commitment to learning and improvement, they provide powerful examples for others to follow. For instance, a teacher who shares their own experiences of overcoming difficulties and striving for personal growth can inspire students to adopt a similar approach to their own challenges. Modelling a growth mindset involves not only demonstrating resilience and a willingness to learn but also encouraging others to embrace these values. By setting an example, leaders and educators can foster a culture of growth and continuous development.

Conclusion

Cultivating a growth mindset, as outlined in Carol Dweck's *Mindset*, involves adopting a set of practices and attitudes that emphasize the potential for growth and improvement. By embracing challenges, learning from criticism, celebrating effort, and viewing failures as opportunities for learning, individuals can foster a mindset that supports personal and professional development. Techniques such as using the word "yet," setting learning goals, transforming self-talk, and modelling a growth mindset are all integral to this process. Through these strategies, individuals can shift their perspective from one of fixed limitations to one of boundless potential, ultimately leading to greater success and fulfilment in various aspects of life.

Dr. Carol Dweck's insights distinctly illuminate how adopting a growth mindset contrasts with a static or fixed mindset. By emphasizing the dynamic nature of abilities and potential, she delineates how those with a growth mindset perceive challenges as opportunities for development, whereas a fixed mindset views them as insurmountable barriers. This distinction clarifies how embracing a growth mindset not only fosters resilience and learning but also differentiates between proactive engagement with opportunities and a static approach that limits personal and professional growth. Thus, her observations elegantly underscore the transformative power of mindset in shaping one's approach to life's challenges and opportunities.

Another example of how a book has the potential to build resilience and fortitude to be the best would be

Can't Hurt Me by David Goggins. David Goggins' *Can't Hurt Me* is a compelling testament to the strength of the human spirit and the pursuit of mental fortitude. While many readers have engaged with this powerful narrative, drawing initial motivation and inspiration, the challenge often lies in sustaining that momentum. Readers may find themselves invigorated and driven to implement Goggins' principles in their lives, only to experience a gradual decline in their efforts as time progresses. This ephemeral burst of motivation, though potent, frequently lacks the enduring impact needed to catalyze lasting change. The true essence of Goggins' message lies not merely in the temporary surge of inspiration but in the consistent, disciplined application of his teachings. To effectuate genuine transformation, one must transcend the initial enthusiasm and embed these principles deeply into daily practice. By cultivating persistence and unwavering commitment, readers can transform the initial motivation into a resilient, enduring mindset that fosters sustained growth and personal evolution. Thus, the key to leveraging *Can't Hurt Me* lies in translating its motivational power into a long-term commitment to self-discipline and mental resilience.

So you see, in the end, to cultivate mental fortitude and embody the growth mindset synonymous with champions, the ultimate recipe for success lies in a harmonious triad of repetition, literary engagement, and pragmatic implementation. These elements, though seemingly straightforward, converge to form the bedrock of a resilient and evolving mindset that transcends mere motivation and forges lasting change.

Repetition stands as the cornerstone of mental fortitude. Much like the disciplined athlete who trains tirelessly to perfect their craft, repetition engrains habits and fortifies the mind against the vicissitudes of adversity. The process of repetitive practice, whether in the realm of physical endurance or cognitive endeavour, gradually transforms initial effort into an ingrained part of one's character. This principle is evident in the transformative journeys of many luminaries who, through relentless repetition, have sculpted their paths to greatness. Such persistence is not merely about enduring the grind; it is about creating an unassailable mental framework where discipline becomes second nature, and challenges are met with unwavering resolve.

Books, those venerable repositories of human wisdom and experience, offer a profound catalyst for mental fortitude. Engaging with literature, particularly texts that challenge and expand one's intellectual and emotional boundaries, cultivates a rich, fertile ground for personal growth. The insights gleaned from books such as Carol Dweck's *Mindset* and David Goggins' *Can't Hurt Me* provide invaluable perspectives and strategies for developing a growth mindset. Through the lens of these literary works, readers can explore the nuanced dynamics of perseverance, resilience, and self-improvement. Books serve as both a beacon and a blueprint, illuminating the path to mental fortitude with their accumulated wisdom and tested principles. However, it is not enough to merely peruse these texts; the true value lies in internalizing their teachings and allowing them to permeate one's approach to life and its myriad challenges.

Implementation represents the practical execution of the insights garnered from both repetitive practice and literary study. It is within the realm of implementation that theoretical knowledge is transmuted into tangible outcomes. The principles learned from books and the habits forged through repetition must be actively applied to real-world scenarios to effectuate genuine change. Implementation requires a concerted effort to translate abstract concepts into actionable strategies and to integrate these strategies into daily routines. It is in this practical application that the growth mindset truly takes root, allowing individuals to navigate obstacles with enhanced resilience and to continually evolve in their pursuit of excellence.

Together, these elements—repetition, books, and implementation—intertwine to create a robust framework for mental fortitude. Repetition instils the necessary discipline and resilience; books provide the intellectual and emotional tools to guide this development; and implementation bridges the gap between knowledge and practice, ensuring that insights are effectively utilized. This triadic approach fosters a mindset akin to that of champions, where mental strength is not merely an aspirational ideal but a tangible reality shaped by deliberate and consistent effort.

In essence, the journey to building mental fortitude and embracing a growth mindset is one of continual refinement and integration. It demands an ongoing commitment to repetition, a voracious appetite for knowledge through books, and a rigorous application of learned principles. By harmonizing these elements, individuals can forge an indomitable mindset, resilient and adaptive, capable of navigating the complexities of life with the poise and determination of a true champion.

Chapter 2: Courage and Leadership

"One of the things that psychotherapists have realised in the last 60 years is that if you can get people to voluntarily confront the things that disturb them and compel them into paralysis and avoidance and possibly even tyranny, the braver and healthier they become. If you gaze upon what terrifies you, long enough and hard enough and with enough diligence, you don't see death and destruction, but the possibility of renewal and rebirth because that's the spirit that is called out of you if you're courageous enough to confront the terrible realities of life"

- Jordan Peterson

Definition and Nature of Courage and Leadership

Understand that, courage and leadership emerge as twin pillars, each interwoven with the other to form the foundation of transformative action and enduring influence. To grasp their essence, one must delve into the labyrinthine interplay between these concepts, exploring their philosophical depths and psychological underpinnings. Courage, in its most profound articulation, is not merely the absence of fear but the audacious resolve to confront and transcend the myriad terrors that lie in wait. Leadership, conversely, is the art of guiding and inspiring others towards a collective vision, often through turbulent seas and uncharted territories. When interlaced, courage and leadership reveal themselves as a singular force—one that empowers individuals to navigate the complexities of existence and to forge pathways where none previously existed.

Conceptual Foundations

To embark upon an exploration of courage and leadership is to engage in a journey through the shadowy realms of human psychology and philosophy. Courage, in its most elemental form, can be understood as the fortitude to face the unknown, to grapple with one's fears, and to persist in the face of adversity. It is a virtue that has captivated the minds of philosophers and scholars throughout history, from Aristotle's ethical discussions to Nietzsche's concept of the Übermensch. In the realm of psychological inquiry, courage is often dissected into its constituent elements: the ability to confront fear, the resilience to withstand hardship, and the audacity to take risks.

Leadership, while similarly exalted, is distinguished by its focus on guiding and influencing others. It involves the capacity to articulate a compelling vision, to galvanize support, and to steer a collective towards a shared goal. The intersection of courage and leadership becomes apparent when one considers that effective leadership often necessitates a courageous stance. Leaders must not only confront their own fears and uncertainties but also inspire others to do the same. This symbiotic relationship between courage and leadership is both a practical necessity and a philosophical ideal, reflecting the complex interplay of inner strength and external influence.

Philosophically, courage is often juxtaposed with its antithesis, cowardice, highlighting its role in ethical and moral considerations. The ancient Greeks revered courage as a cardinal virtue, integral to the development of a noble character. For Aristotle, courage was the mean between recklessness and cowardice, a balanced response to fear that allowed for virtuous action. In modern psychological terms, courage is seen as a dynamic interplay between emotional regulation and cognitive appraisal. It involves not merely the suppression of fear but the active reconfiguration of one's understanding of risk and challenge.

Historical Perspectives

The annals of history are replete with figures whose lives exemplify the profound synergy between courage and leadership. These individuals, through their actions and decisions, have etched indelible marks upon the canvas of human history, embodying the quintessence of these virtues in their respective eras.

In the realm of antiquity, few exemplify the intersection of courage and leadership as vividly as Alexander the Great. The Macedonian conqueror's audacious campaigns across the known world were marked by a blend of fearless ambition and strategic acumen. Alexander's ability to inspire his troops and lead them through perilous campaigns speaks to a profound understanding of the interplay between personal courage and leadership. His legacy, immortalized in the annals of history, underscores how courage, when coupled with visionary leadership, can reshape the course of civilizations.

Turning to the Renaissance, the figure of Leonardo da Vinci emerges as a paragon of courage and leadership in the realms of art and science. Da Vinci's relentless pursuit of knowledge and innovation, despite the societal constraints of his time, exemplifies the courage to challenge conventional wisdom and to pioneer new frontiers. His leadership in the intellectual domain, through his revolutionary ideas and contributions, underscores how courage can manifest in the pursuit of knowledge and the fostering of creativity.

In the more recent past, the life of Nelson Mandela offers a poignant illustration of courage and leadership amidst profound adversity. Mandela's unwavering commitment to justice and equality, despite enduring decades of imprisonment and personal hardship, exemplifies moral courage of the highest order. His leadership in the struggle against apartheid and his subsequent efforts to forge a reconciliatory path for South Africa highlight the transformative power of courage in effecting societal change. Mandela's legacy is a testament to the enduring impact of courageous leadership in overcoming entrenched injustices and fostering a vision of unity and reconciliation.

The 20th century also provides a compelling case in the figure of Winston Churchill, whose leadership during the tumultuous years of World War II was marked by a combination of resolute courage and strategic foresight. Churchill's defiant stance against the encroaching forces of tyranny and his ability to inspire a nation through the dark days of conflict underscore the essential role of courage in leadership. His speeches and decisions, delivered under the shadow of imminent danger, reflect the profound intersection of personal bravery and public responsibility.

In the realm of science and exploration, figures such as Marie Curie exemplify how courage can drive groundbreaking discoveries. Curie's pioneering work in radioactivity, achieved despite significant personal and professional risks, highlights the intersection of intellectual courage and scientific leadership. Her dedication to advancing scientific knowledge, despite the dangers and challenges associated with her research, underscores how courage can propel individuals to achieve extraordinary feats and contribute profoundly to human understanding.

The Interplay of Courage and Leadership

In examining the intersection of courage and leadership, one uncovers a dynamic interplay that transcends mere theoretical constructs. The integration of courage into leadership practices manifests as a catalyst for transformative action and visionary outcomes. Leaders who embody courage inspire others to embrace risk, challenge the status quo, and pursue goals with unwavering determination. This synergy between inner fortitude and outward influence is not merely an abstract ideal but a practical reality that shapes the course of history and the evolution of societies.

The philosophical underpinnings of courage and leadership reflect a deeper understanding of human potential and the capacity for greatness. Courage, as an inner strength, enables individuals to confront their fears and pursue their goals with conviction. Leadership, as an outward expression, harnesses this courage to guide and inspire others towards a shared vision. Together, they form a powerful force for change, capable of overcoming obstacles and achieving extraordinary outcomes.

As one navigates the complex terrain of courage and leadership, it becomes evident that these qualities are not static attributes but dynamic forces that evolve through experience and application. The historical examples of Alexander the Great, Leonardo da Vinci, Nelson Mandela, Winston Churchill, and Marie Curie provide vivid illustrations of how courage and leadership intersect and complement each other. Their legacies, etched into the annals of history, serve as enduring symbols of the transformative power of these virtues.

In conclusion, the definition and nature of courage and leadership reveal a profound and intricate relationship that transcends mere definitions. Courage, as a personal virtue, and leadership, as a guiding force, intertwine to create a dynamic interplay that shapes the course of human endeavour. By examining the historical perspectives and philosophical foundations of these concepts, one gains a deeper appreciation for their significance and impact. The exploration of courage and leadership, therefore, offers a compelling insight into the essence of human greatness and the transformative potential of these intertwined virtues.

> There is no deed in this life so impossible that you cannot do it. Your whole life should be lived as a heroic deed
>
> - Leo Tolstoy

It was only recently that Stoicism first graced my awareness, introduced to me through Ryan Holiday's illuminating work, *The Obstacle is the Way*. Initially, the principles of Stoic philosophy eluded my understanding, their nuances seeming impenetrable. However, with repeated readings, the fog gradually lifted, revealing profound insights and new interpretations of Stoicism. My engagement with Holiday's teachings deepened, leading me to follow his every discourse and presence, particularly on social media.

As I immersed myself further into Stoic ideologies, I found myself transformed. The ability to maintain composure in the face of minor irritations became second nature. My self-control improved markedly, and a genuine sense of happiness and inner fortitude emerged. I became emboldened, prepared to confront any challenge with equanimity and resilience. Moreover, Stoicism did not solely reshape my mindset; it harmoniously integrated with the wisdom of my own religious scriptures. Allow me to illuminate the essence of what I have learned, revealing how these philosophical and spiritual insights have collectively enriched and fortified my approach to life.

My Reflections from the Stoic Philosophy about Courage

In the grand theatre of human experience, courage is the paramount virtue, one that transmutes mere existence into a life of profound significance and resolute purpose. To ascend to the pinnacle of courage is to embark upon a transformative journey, where fear is confronted not with mere bravery but with the dignified calm of the Stoic sage. Stoic philosophy, with its rich tapestry of ancient wisdom, offers an exquisite and enigmatic guide to cultivating superlative courage. This treatise explores the enigmatic allure of Stoic courage through a series of illuminating examples and timeless stories, weaving together the threads of philosophy and practice to reveal the path to true fortitude.

The Stoic Foundations of Courage

At the heart of Stoic philosophy lies the distinction between what is within our control and what is not. This fundamental principle, expounded by the Stoics, forms the bedrock of their approach to courage. Courage, in the Stoic sense, is not the absence of fear but the rational response to the inevitability of adversity. It is a measured embrace of challenges, guided by reason and virtue rather than impulse and emotion.

The Enigmatic Teachings of Epictetus

Epictetus, the renowned Stoic philosopher, elucidated the nature of courage through his reflections on personal responsibility and the nature of freedom. His teachings underscore the idea that true courage is derived from the mastery of one's internal state rather than external circumstances.

One of the most poignant examples of Epictetus' philosophy in action is encapsulated in his discourse on the nature of adversity. He recounts a vivid tale of a man who, upon facing an impending danger, demonstrates the quintessence of Stoic courage. When the man is threatened by a formidable adversary, he remains undaunted, not because he is unafraid, but because he has cultivated an inner detachment from the outcomes. He understands that the only domain within his control is his response to the situation, and thus, he meets the challenge with calm resolve and unshakeable dignity.

Epictetus also provides a rich metaphor through the concept of the "inner citadel," a fortified bastion within each individual's psyche. This inner fortress, impervious to external assaults, is the wellspring of Stoic courage. The metaphor elucidates that true fortitude is achieved not through the suppression of fear but through the cultivation of an inviolable inner strength. By reinforcing this citadel through reasoned reflection and disciplined practice, one can attain a state of courage that remains unperturbed by the vicissitudes of life.

Seneca's Resilient Stoicism
Seneca, another luminary of Stoic thought, offers profound insights into the nature of courage through his essays and letters. His reflections on adversity and the human condition provide a compelling narrative on the role of courage in the face of existential challenges.

In his celebrated work, *On the Shortness of Life*, Seneca illuminates the essence of courage by examining the ephemeral nature of human existence. He argues that courage is not merely about confronting external threats but also about living a life that is fully engaged and authentically aligned with one's values. Seneca posits that true courage involves the conscious embrace of mortality and the pursuit of a life lived with purpose and integrity. He recounts the story of a noble Roman who, upon receiving a terminal diagnosis, faces his fate with a serenity that transcends fear. This stoic composure, Seneca asserts, is the hallmark of genuine courage, reflecting an acceptance of the impermanence of life and an unwavering commitment to personal virtue. Seneca also offers a compelling narrative through his reflections on the nature of suffering and endurance. He recounts the tale of a prisoner subjected to brutal conditions who remains resolute and undaunted. The prisoner's courage is not derived from the absence of physical pain but from a profound inner strength that allows him to maintain his dignity and composure. This story serves as a testament to the Stoic ideal that true courage is an internal quality, a resilience that defies the external circumstances and remains steadfast in the face of adversity.

Marcus Aurelius and the Art of Inner Strength
Marcus Aurelius, the Stoic emperor, provides a rich source of wisdom on courage through his *Meditations*. His reflections, penned during the tumultuous years of his reign, offer an intimate

glimpse into the mind of a leader who grappled with the challenges of power, responsibility, and existential uncertainty.

In his meditations, Marcus Aurelius often returns to the theme of courage as an inner fortitude that is cultivated through philosophical reflection and self-discipline. He emphasizes the importance of confronting one's fears with reasoned detachment, recognizing that true courage involves an acceptance of the transitory nature of life and the impermanence of all external circumstances. Marcus Aurelius writes, "The impediment to action advances action. What stands in the way becomes the way." This poignant insight reveals the Stoic belief that courage is not merely about overcoming obstacles but about embracing them as opportunities for growth and self-improvement.

Marcus Aurelius also provides a vivid portrayal of courage through his reflections on the nature of duty and responsibility. He recounts the trials of leadership and the challenges of maintaining integrity amidst the demands of power. His writings reveal a profound understanding of courage as the ability to uphold one's principles and fulfill one's responsibilities with unwavering dedication, despite the personal cost. The emperor's meditations reflect a deep-seated commitment to the Stoic ideal of living in accordance with virtue, embodying a form of courage that transcends the superficial and touches upon the profound essence of ethical living.

The Alchemical Transmutation of Fear

The Stoic philosophy of courage can be likened to an alchemical process, wherein the raw material of fear is transmuted into the gold of inner strength. This transformative journey is not achieved through denial or suppression but through the conscious and deliberate engagement with one's fears and anxieties. By embracing the Stoic principles of rationality and virtue, individuals can effectuate a profound change in their relationship with fear, converting it from a source of paralysis into a wellspring of resilience.
The process of this alchemical transformation involves a series of deliberate steps. Firstly, one must cultivate an awareness of the nature of fear, recognizing it as a natural and inevitable aspect of the human condition. Stoic philosophy teaches that fear is not an enemy to be vanquished but a signal to be understood. By engaging with fear through rational reflection and philosophical inquiry, individuals can gain insight into its origins and manifestations.
Secondly, the Stoic approach emphasizes the importance of distinguishing between what is within our control and what is not. By focusing on the realm of personal agency and choice, individuals can shift their attention from the external circumstances that provoke fear to the internal responses that can be cultivated. This shift in focus allows for the development of a more resilient and courageous mindset, one that is grounded in the understanding of one's own capacity for action and response.
Finally, the cultivation of courage through Stoic practice involves the conscious and deliberate application of virtue in the face of adversity. Stoic

philosophy teaches that courage is not a passive state but an active engagement with the challenges of life. By embracing the principles of wisdom, justice, and temperance, individuals can navigate the complexities of existence with a sense of purpose and integrity, transforming fear into a catalyst for personal growth and ethical living.

In the enigmatic realms of Stoic philosophy, courage emerges as a profound and multifaceted virtue, one that transcends mere bravery and encompasses a deep-seated resilience and inner strength. Through the teachings of Epictetus, Seneca, and Marcus Aurelius, we gain a rich and nuanced understanding of courage as an internal quality, cultivated through reasoned reflection, philosophical inquiry, and the deliberate application of virtue.

The stories and examples drawn from Stoic philosophy reveal a path to superlative courage, one that involves the alchemical transmutation of fear into inner strength and the conscious embrace of adversity as a means of personal growth. By engaging with these timeless teachings and integrating them into our own lives, we can aspire to a form of courage that is not merely the absence of fear but a profound and enduring resilience that shapes our character and guides our actions.

Thus, the pursuit of Stoic courage invites us to embark upon a transformative journey, one that transcends the superficial and touches upon the profound essence of human greatness. In embracing the principles of Stoic philosophy, we can cultivate a courage that is both elegant and formidable, a courage that reflects the deepest aspirations of the human spirit and the timeless wisdom of the ancients.

These revelations about courage, bravery, fear, and resilience catalyzed my introspective journey towards greater inner fortitude. I embarked on a quest to cultivate a profound sense of courage, learning to navigate the complexities of decision-making with a steadfast resolve. My pursuit was not merely about surface-level bravery but about developing an unwavering strength that enables me to confront life's trials with poise and dignity.

In this quest, I sought to fortify myself emotionally, striving to become so resolute and composed that I could endure loss with a stoic serenity, untouched by tears. This process involved a rigorous self-examination and the deliberate honing of my inner resolve. By embracing these Stoic principles, I endeavoured to build a character that stands resilient in the face of adversity, capable of bearing the weight of sorrow with calm acceptance. This journey has imbued me with the strength to face challenges with a courageous heart and a steadfast spirit, transforming my understanding of personal bravery into a profound inner resilience.

The same transformative journey awaits you. All that is required is the initiative to embark upon it. By embracing the principles of courage, bravery, and resilience, you too can cultivate an inner fortitude that enables you to confront challenges with grace and strength. This journey demands not just passive reflection but active engagement, leading to a profound transformation in how you handle adversity. Take the first step, and the path to enduring courage and steadfast resolve will reveal itself, guiding you towards a more resilient and empowered self.

Part I:

Igniting Courage: Elegy of the Fearless

In our lives, there come moments when we are not merely touched by fear but rather enveloped in its most profound and paralyzing form—terror. This terror, far more insidious than simple dread, grips us with a suffocating intensity that borders on the mortal. It might arise from the crushing weight of obligations that bind us, or perhaps from the capricious whims of fate's cruel design. Sometimes, this terror emerges from an abyss so vast and unfathomable that even the most ardent quest over countless years yields but a mere tremor of progress.

Imagine, if you will, a shadowy expanse that stretches beyond the confines of our understanding, a chasm so deep that no amount of relentless striving can hope to bridge it fully. This is no ordinary fear but a terror that seeps into the very marrow of our existence, a dread that eclipses the mundane apprehensions of everyday life. It is as though we are thrust into a realm where the ordinary rules no longer apply, where our every step is shadowed by an omnipresent sense of foreboding.

The nature of this terror is not always clear-cut; it can stem from the monumental responsibilities that loom over us like an inexorable storm, or from the capricious flotsam and jetsam of life's unpredictable currents. At times, it may even spring from a grand, inscrutable enigma—an overarching question or purpose so vast in its scope that our earnest endeavours to grasp it only stir the surface of its profundity. The pursuit of such an elusive goal becomes a Sisyphean task, where every effort seems but a fleeting whisper against the roaring gale of its enormity.

This experience of terror transcends mere fear, delving into a realm where the boundaries of self and world blur into an indistinct haze. It is as though we are ensnared in a labyrinthine dance with an unfathomable force, where each step forward feels both a triumph and a further entanglement in the web of our own making. The pursuit of understanding or overcoming this terror can become a journey fraught with both magnificence and melancholy—a relentless chase after a mirage that seems to recede with every advance.

Thus, in the face of such profound terror, we stand at the precipice of our own limitations, grappling with the realization that some shadows may never fully recede. The very act of confronting this terror becomes a testament to our resilience, a measure of our courage in the face of an adversary that defies all attempts at resolution. And so, we continue onward, navigating the delicate balance between despair and determination, knowing that the pursuit itself shapes us in ways both visible and arcane.

In the end, it is this enigmatic dance with terror—this intricate interplay of courage and fear—that defines our most profound trials. We confront the unknown, not merely with trepidation but with a fierce and unyielding resolve, understanding that in the deepest shadows, we may discover not just our greatest fears but also our most profound strengths.

In confronting the most harrowing of fears, where terror grips us with an unyielding and relentless grasp, there exists a paradoxical remedy—one that is both simple and profound. The path to overcoming such a formidable adversary does not lie in the ephemeral whims of chance or the transient strategies of the moment. Rather, it is found in the sacred and repetitive cadence of ancient wisdom. Yet, what is this repetition, and where does its true power reside?

The answer lies within the hallowed pages of the Scriptures. These timeless texts, imbued with the essence of divine insight, hold the keys to navigating the labyrinth of our existence. It is not merely the act of repetition itself that holds sway but the profound essence contained within these venerable writings. Through their recitation and reflection, we engage in a ritual that transcends the mundane and touches the ethereal.

The Scriptures, in their myriad forms and interpretations, offer a wellspring of teachings that transcend the temporal and the transient. They are not mere words inked on ancient parchment but are vessels of eternal truth. When we immerse ourselves in their rhythms, we are not simply repeating phrases but weaving ourselves into a grand tapestry of wisdom that has withstood the test of millennia. This repetition becomes a sacred practice, a litany of transformation that molds our very essence and fortifies our spirit.

It is within this repetitive engagement with sacred texts that we discover the tools to not merely endure but to transcend the vicissitudes of life. The teachings contained within these Scriptures are like a compass in the storm, guiding us with unwavering clarity through the darkest of nights. They offer not just solace but a pathway to mastery over the chaotic forces that seek to dismantle our lives.

As we repeat these sacred passages, we embark upon a transformative journey. Each recitation deepens our understanding, each reflection sharpens our resolve. It is through this iterative process that we forge a new narrative for ourselves—one where our lives evolve from mere existence into a tale of triumph and grandeur. Our fears, once overwhelming and insurmountable, begin to recede as we harness the strength derived from this sacred repetition.

The life thus forged is not a trivial chronicle but a saga of courage and transcendence. We become not merely participants in our own stories but the very architects of a legacy that commands respect and admiration. The recurrent engagement with Scripture enables us to confront our deepest fears with a grace that transforms them into stepping stones on the path to personal exaltation.

Thus, the secret to mastering the most brutal fears lies not in ephemeral solutions or transient comforts but in the profound repetition of divine wisdom. Through this sacred practice, we transform our lives from a mere struggle into a grand narrative—a testament to the enduring power of ancient teachings and the unyielding strength they bestow upon us. Our existence, illuminated by the light of these eternal words, becomes a story worth telling and a life worthy of reverence.

Embrace the wisdom of the Bhagavad Gita and unlock your true potential. Face your responsibilities with courage and determination, knowing that every challenge is an opportunity for growth. Let the sacred teachings guide you, transforming your mind into your greatest ally. View each victory and defeat with equal composure, for true strength lies in maintaining inner balance. By embodying these divine principles, you rise above mere existence, becoming a beacon of grace and courage. Your journey of applying these teachings not only earns you respect in this world but also draws you closer to the divine embrace of Shri Bhagawan Himself.

Here are a few shlokas:

कर्मण्येवाधिकारस्ते मा फलेषु कदाचन।
मा कर्मफलहेतुर्भूर्मा ते सङ्गोऽस्त्वकर्मणि॥

Translation: You have the right to perform your prescribed duties, but you are not entitled to the fruits of your actions. Never consider yourself to be the cause of the results of your activities, nor be attached to inaction.

Significance for Courage: The shloka from the Bhagavad Gita embodies profound wisdom on courage and action. This verse advises us to focus solely on our duties without being attached to the outcomes. It emphasizes that our right is only to perform our actions, not to control or be obsessed with the results. This detachment from the fruits of our labour cultivates a courageous mindset, free from the paralyzing fears of success or failure.

By adhering to this principle, one practices a form of inner strength and resilience that transcends the ordinary. It fosters a mindset where actions are driven by duty and righteousness rather than personal gain, embodying true courage. Such an approach ensures that we act with integrity and resolve, unperturbed by external rewards or setbacks. This unwavering commitment to our responsibilities, grounded in the understanding that results are beyond our control, is not only a testament to our personal strength but also aligns with divine virtues. The divine, in turn, honours such steadfastness and selflessness, seeing it as a reflection of the highest moral and spiritual caliber.

यं हि न व्यथयन्त्येते पुरुषं पुरुषर्षभ।
समदुःखसुखं धीरं सोऽमृतत्वाय कल्पते॥

Translation: He who is not disturbed by the incessant flow of desires that enter like rivers into the ocean, which is being filled but is always being still, can alone achieve peace, and not the person who strives to satisfy such desires.

Significance for Courage: The shloka from the Bhagavad Gita highlights the essence of true bravery and courage. It describes a person who remains unperturbed by the dualities of life—joy and sorrow, success and failure. Such a person, who maintains equanimity amidst life's fluctuations, embodies the highest form of inner strength and resilience.

The significance of this verse lies in its portrayal of ideal courage. True bravery is not merely about facing external challenges but about mastering one's internal responses. A person who is steady and composed in the face of both pleasure and pain demonstrates profound inner fortitude. This calmness, or "dhira," reflects a deep understanding and acceptance of the transient nature of worldly experiences.

By achieving such balance, one transcends the limitations of ordinary existence and aligns with a higher, almost divine state of being. This unwavering equanimity earns the highest praise, as it mirrors the divine qualities of stability and detachment. The divine recognizes and honours those who embody this ideal of balanced courage, seeing them as embodiments of eternal wisdom and spiritual grace.

सुखदुःखे समे कृत्वा लाभालाभौ जयाजयौ।
ततो युद्धाय युज्यस्व नैवं पापमवाप्स्यसि॥

Translation: Considering happiness and distress, gain and loss, victory and defeat as equal, engage yourself in the battle. By doing so, you will not incur sin.

Significance for Courage: The shloka from the Bhagavad Gita imparts profound lessons on courage and fortitude. This verse urges us to approach life with equanimity, treating pleasure and pain, success and failure with equal composure. Such an attitude forms the bedrock of true courage.

The essence of this teaching is that true bravery involves maintaining inner balance regardless of external circumstances. By equating joy with sorrow and gain with loss, one cultivates a steadfastness of spirit that remains undisturbed by the shifting tides of fortune. This unwavering resolve empowers us to act with integrity and determination, free from the paralyzing effects of fear or attachment.

In the context of a battle or any challenge, this equanimity ensures that our actions are guided by duty rather than personal gain or loss. When we engage in our responsibilities with this mindset, we transcend the bounds of ordinary human concerns and act from a place of divine clarity. Thus, we are not only courageous but also align ourselves with a higher moral order, earning the divine's approval and reinforcing our path to righteousness.

[NOTE] : I couldn't provide examples from The Quran or The Bible because I do not have the necessary intel for it and also I am a human so a bit lazy as well. Perhaps we can get examples from them in the next book of the series.

The quest for courage and resilience extends beyond celestial wisdom. The Bhagavad Gita, imparted by Shri Bhagawan Himself, offers a transcendent blueprint for fortitude, enshrining divine principles in the realm of human struggle. Yet, while the sacred texts provide a celestial framework, the philosophical pursuit of courage from a mortal perspective unveils a distinct, equally profound path—a journey where human agency and introspective contemplation illuminate the essence of bravery.

Divine philosophy, with its celestial authority, offers an ethereal lens through which courage is understood, emphasizing a transcendental equilibrium amid life's vicissitudes. The teachings advocate a stoic detachment, wherein one's actions are imbued with duty and righteousness, unclouded by the allure of success or the dread of failure. Such divine guidance provides an imperishable foundation, anchoring individuals in an unwavering commitment to their responsibilities.

However, the human experience, rich with its own tapestry of struggle and insight, reveals a nuanced and intimately personal exploration of courage. Mortals, too, possess the ability to wield courage, not merely as a reflection of divine will but as a tangible force that can be cultivated and propagated within the confines of human reality. This mortal perspective on courage encompasses a philosophical dimension that is as profound as it is accessible, rooted in the existential experiences and trials that shape human lives.

Consider the existentialist viewpoint, which delves into the heart of human freedom and responsibility. Existentialist thinkers like Jean-Paul Sartre and Friedrich Nietzsche challenge us to confront the absurdity of existence and the inherent freedom of choice. Sartre's assertion that "existence precedes essence" places the burden of creating meaning squarely on the shoulders of individuals. Courage, in this context, becomes the act of embracing one's freedom and responsibility, despite the inherent uncertainty and meaninglessness of the universe. It is a raw, unadorned bravery that emerges from acknowledging the void and choosing to act with authenticity and purpose, even when the path ahead is obscured by existential doubt.

Nietzsche, with his concept of the "Übermensch" or "Overman," further expands this notion, advocating for a revaluation of values and the creation of one's own destiny. For Nietzsche, courage is not merely about facing external challenges but about transcending conventional moral constraints and forging new paths. The Übermensch embodies a fearless, self-affirming spirit, capable of redefining existence on their own terms. This philosophical courage is a testament to human potential, where individuals harness their willpower to overcome societal norms and personal limitations, sculpting their own destiny amidst the chaos of existence.

Turning to the Stoic philosophers, we encounter a different yet equally compelling dimension of courage. Stoicism, as articulated by Marcus Aurelius, Seneca, and Epictetus, advocates for a form of inner resilience that remains impervious to external fluctuations. According to Stoic thought, true courage involves cultivating an inner fortitude that enables one to face adversity with equanimity. The Stoic ideal of "apatheia," or emotional detachment, is not about suppressing emotions but about mastering them. This philosophical approach to courage emphasizes the importance of rational control and acceptance of what is beyond our influence. It is a profound embrace of inner tranquility, where courage manifests as a steadfast adherence to virtue and wisdom, irrespective of external circumstances.

In the realm of modern existential and psychological philosophy, the concept of "authenticity" further enriches our understanding of courage. The existentialist Carl Rogers, for instance, highlights the significance of being true to oneself as a core aspect of courage. Authenticity, in this sense, involves confronting one's fears and insecurities, embracing vulnerability, and living in accordance with one's true values. This form of courage is deeply personal and transformative, requiring individuals to transcend societal expectations and inner conflicts to achieve a genuine alignment with their innermost selves.

Moreover, the psychological perspective on courage, as explored by figures like Viktor Frankl, provides additional layers of insight. Frankl's exploration of "logotherapy" reveals that courage often emerges from the search for meaning in the face of suffering. According to Frankl, even in the direst of circumstances, individuals can find a profound sense of purpose and resilience. Courage, in this framework, is not just about enduring hardship but about finding significance and striving for a higher purpose amidst the trials of existence. It is a testament to the human spirit's capacity to transcend suffering and embrace a purposeful life.

In synthesizing these philosophical perspectives, we arrive at a rich, multifaceted understanding of courage that transcends divine and mortal realms. While divine philosophy provides a celestial guidepost for righteous action and detachment, mortal perspectives on courage offer a tangible and deeply human exploration of bravery. Whether through existential freedom, Stoic resilience, or the quest for authenticity and meaning, courage emerges as a multifaceted virtue that can be cultivated and wielded by individuals in their own unique contexts.

Ultimately, the philosophical exploration of courage reveals that it is not a static or monolithic trait but a dynamic and evolving aspect of the human condition. It is an intricate dance between facing external challenges and mastering internal conflicts, a journey that requires both divine guidance and human introspection. By embracing this dual perspective, we gain a deeper appreciation of courage as a force that transcends the boundaries of both the divine and the mortal, illuminating the path to resilience and strength in the ever-unfolding drama of human existence.

But courage transcends the mere grasp of abstract philosophies and incisive reasoning; it is an exquisite ballet of embodying these profound concepts and translating them into tangible deeds that illuminate the world's shadows. It is not simply the theoretical acquaintance with the grand ideals that beckon to the soul, but rather the audacious spirit to enkindle those ideals into the very fabric of existence. The essence of valour lies in the alchemy of thought and action, where abstract musings metamorphose into acts of transformative grace. To truly epitomize courage is to weave the threads of philosophical wisdom into the tapestry of daily life, to carve paths through the morass of inertia and indifference with a resolute heart. It is an elegant symphony of intention and execution, a dance where the ethereal musings of the mind are married to the palpable actions of the body. This sublime harmony does not merely echo through the corridors of the intellect but reverberates in the realm of the tangible, where the quintessence of bravery is etched into the very contours of our shared reality. In this alchemical fusion, courage emerges not just as a virtue but as a transformative force that, through its luminous essence, seeks to sculpt a more enlightened and harmonious world.

So how might we cultivate the essence of courage within ourselves, armed with a steadfast heart and profound wisdom? To cultivate courage and resilience, the simplest answer might be to practice it, as we've discussed. This approach, while a good starting point, raises further questions about where and when one should practice. These questions are inherently subjective, as there is no universal blueprint for forging bravery. Each individual's path will vary, and what works for one person might not suit another. Yet, there are unconventional and inspiring methods drawn from the legacies of warriors and cultures throughout history that offer profound insights into this journey.

Consider the Vikings, those legendary seafarers of the North. Their approach to building courage was rooted in a culture of both myth and reality. The sagas tell of fierce battles and epic voyages, but they also reveal a deeper practice: the preparation for the inevitable uncertainties of life. Vikings embraced the philosophy of "Valkyries," warrior maidens who chose those who would live or die in battle. They believed in facing their fears with a resolute heart, understanding that every challenge was a step toward earning their place in the hall of the gods. To forge courage like the Vikings, one must embrace the unknown, face their fears head-on, and prepare oneself mentally and physically for life's battles, understanding that courage is not the absence of fear but the will to move forward despite it.

Similarly, the ancient Spartans offer another perspective. Spartan training was legendary for its rigor and discipline. From a young age, Spartan children underwent intense training designed not only to build physical strength but also to instill resilience and courage. This training was harsh, involving rigorous exercises, mock battles, and a philosophy that prized endurance and bravery above all else. Spartans learned that true courage came from pushing past their limits and enduring hardships. They understood that resilience was forged in the crucible of difficulty, and every trial was an opportunity to strengthen one's spirit. To follow the Spartan path is to embrace discomfort and challenge as essential components of personal growth, seeking out experiences that test and fortify your resolve.

In a different cultural context, the warriors of the Mahabharata, such as Arjuna and Bhima, offer a rich example of courage and resilience. The Mahabharata, an epic that intertwines the fates of gods and men, presents a complex picture of bravery. Arjuna's struggle on the battlefield of Kurukshetra, faced with moral dilemmas and fears, highlights an important aspect of courage: the ability to confront inner conflicts and uncertainties. Arjuna's journey involved not only physical battles but also a deep spiritual quest for understanding his duty and purpose. The lesson here is that true courage involves grappling with one's inner fears and moral quandaries, seeking clarity and purpose amidst chaos. To emulate the Mahabharata warriors is to engage in deep introspection, aligning one's actions with a sense of greater purpose and duty.

Drawing from these diverse historical examples, forging courage and resilience involves several key practices:

1. **Embrace the Unknown:** Like the Vikings, face the uncertainties of life with a mindset that every challenge is an opportunity. Rather than avoiding risks, lean into them and prepare

yourself mentally for the unpredictability of existence.
2. **Endure Hardship:** Following the Spartan example, seek out experiences that push your boundaries. Embrace discomfort as a pathway to growth, understanding that resilience is built through enduring and overcoming adversity.
3. **Confront Inner Conflicts:** Inspired by the Mahabharata warriors, engage in self-reflection to address internal fears and moral dilemmas. Cultivate inner strength by aligning your actions with a sense of purpose and confronting the deeper questions of your existence.
4. **Practice Daily Resilience:** Incorporate small, manageable challenges into your daily routine. Just as the Spartans trained relentlessly, engage in regular practices that test and build your resilience, from physical exercises to mental challenges.
5. **Seek Mentors and Role Models:** Surround yourself with individuals who embody courage and resilience. Learning from those who have faced significant trials can offer valuable insights and inspiration.
6. **Cultivate a Supportive Community**: Like the camaraderie of Viking warriors or Spartan soldiers, build a network of support. Share your challenges with others and draw strength from mutual encouragement and shared experiences.

7. **Reflect and Adapt:** Regularly assess your progress and adapt your strategies. Reflect on your experiences and adjust your approach based on what you learn about yourself and the challenges you face.

In conclusion, while the quest to cultivate courage and resilience is profoundly personal and varies from one individual to another, certain enduring principles remain constant. The essence of bravery is shaped by these principles, and those who align themselves with them are destined to triumph. The one who embraces and adapts to these timeless truths will ultimately emerge victorious, having forged a path of unyielding strength and unwavering resolve.

Part II:

Critical Thinking: First Aspect Of Leadership

> No man is free who is not a master of himself
>
> - Epictetus

Thinking critically is a fundamental skill that empowers individuals to analyze and evaluate information with discernment and depth. It involves a deliberate and systematic approach to understanding and interpreting the world, rather than passively accepting information or relying on intuition alone. ***At its core, critical thinking is about questioning assumptions, seeking evidence, and evaluating arguments in a reasoned and objective manner.***

To engage in critical thinking, one must first recognize the value of questioning. This means not taking information at face value but probing deeper to understand its origins, context, and validity. ***Critical thinkers ask questions such as: What evidence supports this claim? Are there alternative viewpoints? What are the potential biases influencing this perspective?*** By addressing these questions, individuals can uncover underlying assumptions and assess the strength of the arguments presented.

Another key aspect of critical thinking is the evaluation of evidence. This involves scrutinizing the credibility and relevance of sources, as well as the consistency and reliability of the information provided. It requires **distinguishing between well-supported facts and mere opinions or conjecture.** Critical thinkers weigh the evidence carefully, considering its implications and how it fits into the broader context.

Moreover, critical thinking involves recognizing and mitigating cognitive biases. These are systematic errors in thinking that can distort judgment and decision-making. By being aware of biases such as confirmation bias or groupthink, individuals can strive for more objective and balanced assessments.

Ultimately, critical thinking enhances decision-making and problem-solving by fostering a deeper understanding of complex issues. It equips individuals with the tools to navigate uncertainty, challenge prevailing narratives, and arrive at well-reasoned conclusions. In a world overflowing with information and competing perspectives, critical thinking is indispensable for making informed choices and engaging meaningfully with diverse viewpoints.

Critical thinkers navigate the labyrinth of competing viewpoints with finesse and discernment, ultimately arriving at conclusions that are both nuanced and well-founded. To illustrate this process, we can examine the approaches of Jordan Peterson and Dr. S. Jaishankar, two prominent figures known for their rigorous analytical frameworks and profound insights. Their methods exemplify how one can synthesize multiple perspectives into coherent, reasoned conclusions.

Jordan Peterson offers a compelling model of critical thinking through his extensive work in psychology and his public discourse. Peterson emphasizes the importance of confronting the complexities of life with intellectual integrity and personal responsibility. In his book *"12 Rules for Life: An Antidote to Chaos,"* he articulates that "***To stand up straight with your shoulders back is to accept the burden of being.***" This metaphorical posture is not merely about physical alignment but symbolizes an approach to dealing with competing ideas and viewpoints with confidence and composure.

Peterson's critical thinking process involves several stages. First, he advocates for a meticulous examination of the foundational principles underlying various arguments. For instance, in his discussions on political and social issues, Peterson often begins by deconstructing ideologies to reveal their core assumptions. He argues, "***The first step toward knowledge is the recognition of the*** *possibility of error."* This statement underscores his belief that acknowledging the fallibility of one's beliefs is crucial for arriving at a more accurate understanding.

Moreover, Peterson employs a dialectical method, engaging with opposing viewpoints to test the robustness of his own ideas. He often debates with those who hold contrary opinions, using these exchanges as a crucible for refining his arguments. This method is evident in his dialogues on platforms such as *The Joe Rogan Experience,* where he systematically addresses objections and counterarguments, thus demonstrating a commitment to intellectual rigour and openness.

Dr. S. Jaishankar, India's External Affairs Minister, exemplifies a different yet complementary approach to critical thinking, particularly in the realm of international relations. His analyses are shaped by a deep understanding of geopolitical dynamics and cultural contexts. In his book *"The India Way: Strategies for an Uncertain World,"* Dr Jaishankar posits that *"**The future of global order will depend on how we manage the interplay between power and principles.**"* This perspective highlights the complexity of global issues, where multiple viewpoints and interests intersect.

Dr. Jaishankar's critical thinking is characterized by a pragmatic approach to diplomacy and strategy. He emphasizes the importance of context and historical continuity in understanding international relations. For instance, he often reflects on India's position within the global landscape, considering both historical grievances and current strategic interests. In a lecture at the Indian Council of World Affairs, he remarked, "History is a guide, but not a straitjacket." This statement reflects his belief that while historical patterns provide valuable insights, they should not constrain contemporary decision-making.

Dr. Jaishankar's method involves a comprehensive analysis of historical and cultural contexts to navigate complex global issues. He integrates diverse perspectives by examining the strategic interests of various stakeholders and the potential implications of different courses of action. His approach is both analytical and diplomatic, aiming to balance competing interests while pursuing pragmatic solutions.

The strategies which complement the articulation of figures like Jordan Peterson and Dr S. Jaishankar, in my interpretation, are the following:

1. **Principled Inquiry**: Peterson's approach begins with a deep dive into the principles underlying various arguments. By understanding the foundational beliefs driving different perspectives, he is able to evaluate their merits and limitations. Similarly, Dr. Jaishankar examines historical and cultural

contexts to understand the motivations and strategies of various global actors.

2. **Dialectical Engagement**: Peterson engages in rigorous debates and discussions, exposing his ideas to critique and refining them based on feedback. This dialectical process allows him to test his arguments against opposing viewpoints and strengthen his conclusions. Dr. Jaishankar, while less public in debate, engages with international counterparts and stakeholders to understand diverse perspectives and negotiate complex issues.

3. **Contextual Analysis**: Dr. Jaishankar's critical thinking involves a detailed analysis of the historical and cultural contexts that shape international relations. By understanding the broader context, he can navigate competing interests and propose strategies that are both informed and pragmatic. Peterson also considers context, particularly in his psychological and philosophical analyses, to ensure that his conclusions are grounded in a comprehensive understanding of the issues.

4. **Intellectual Humility**: Both thinkers exhibit a form of intellectual humility, acknowledging the limitations of their knowledge and the possibility of error. Peterson's recognition of

fallibility and Dr. Jaishankar's acknowledgment of historical complexities reflect a willingness to adapt and refine their viewpoints in light of new evidence or insights.

5. **Integration of Insights**: The final step in their process involves integrating insights from various perspectives to form a coherent conclusion. Peterson synthesizes his understanding of psychological theories, philosophical principles, and practical experiences to articulate his viewpoints. Dr. Jaishankar integrates historical analysis, strategic considerations, and diplomatic insights to navigate complex global issues.

In conclusion, critical thinkers like Jordan Peterson and Dr. S. Jaishankar exemplify how to navigate multiple viewpoints with sophistication and depth. Their methods—rooted in principled inquiry, dialectical engagement, contextual analysis, intellectual humility, and the integration of diverse insights—demonstrate how to arrive at well-reasoned conclusions in a complex and multifaceted world. By employing these strategies, one can adeptly navigate the intricate terrain of competing ideas and make informed, nuanced judgments.

In Chapter 1, we touched on the foundational concepts of Emotional Regulation and Communication, setting the stage for deeper exploration. But the journey doesn't end there. Prepare for an in-depth examination of these crucial traits and more in the forthcoming prequel to this book. Scheduled for release soon, this prequel promises to delve into twelve transformative qualities that define exceptional leadership. With insights and practical strategies, it will illuminate how these traits can be harnessed to elevate your leadership skills and drive meaningful change. Stay tuned for an engaging exploration that will equip you with the tools to lead with unparalleled effectiveness and inspiration.

Thinking critically is certainly no child's play. It's a skill that demands depth and nuance, shaping our understanding of the world around us. While critical thinking is essential for effective leadership, it is not the sole ingredient. Much like the complexity of a person transcends mere skin and organs, the essence of good leadership encompasses various dimensions.

Beyond critical thinking, effective leaders must embody empathy, integrity, and vision. Empathy allows leaders to connect with their team on a human level, fostering trust and collaboration. Integrity builds credibility, ensuring that leaders are seen as trustworthy and principled. Meanwhile, a clear vision guides the leader and their team toward a shared purpose, inspiring collective effort.

Moreover, adaptability is crucial; the ability to pivot in response to changing circumstances and to embrace innovation ensures relevance in an ever-evolving landscape. Emotional intelligence also plays a pivotal role, equipping leaders to navigate interpersonal dynamics with grace and understanding.

Thus, while critical thinking lays an important foundation, the tapestry of good leadership is woven from various threads—each vital to creating a harmonious and effective whole. A truly great leader harmonizes these qualities, creating an environment where others can thrive and contribute meaningfully to the collective journey. In this way, leadership becomes not just a role, but an art form, one that resonates deeply with those it touches.

Numerous books have emerged that not only promote this skill but also inspire readers to engage deeply with the world around them. Here, we explore some of the most influential works that exemplify critical thinking and encourage its cultivation.

1. "Thinking, Fast and Slow" by Daniel Kahneman

Nobel laureate Daniel Kahneman's "Thinking, Fast and Slow" is a profound exploration of the dual systems of thought that govern our decision-making processes. Kahneman distinguishes between the intuitive, quick responses of System 1 and the deliberate, analytical approaches of System 2.

Through a rich tapestry of research findings, anecdotes, and psychological insights, he demonstrates how our minds can lead us astray, prompting readers to critically evaluate their thinking patterns and biases. This book serves as a call to awareness, urging readers to question their automatic responses and consider more reflective approaches in their judgments.

2. "The Demon-Haunted World: Science as a Candle in the Dark" by Carl Sagan

In "The Demon-Haunted World," Carl Sagan passionately defends the scientific method and critical thinking as vital tools in combating superstition and pseudoscience. Sagan's accessible writing encourages readers to embrace skepticism and inquiry, equipping them with the tools to discern fact from fiction. By illustrating the dangers of unexamined beliefs, he inspires readers to cultivate a questioning mindset and to seek evidence before accepting claims. His discussions on the importance of scientific literacy are a clarion call for fostering critical thought in a world often clouded by misinformation.

3. "How to Read a Book" by Mortimer Adler and Charles Van Doren

"How to Read a Book" is not merely a guide to reading; it is a manifesto for engaging with texts in a thoughtful and analytical manner. Mortimer Adler and Charles Van Doren outline various levels of reading and provide strategies for extracting meaning and insights from complex works. This book encourages readers to approach literature with curiosity and critical engagement, fostering a deeper understanding of ideas and arguments. By emphasizing the importance of active reading, it serves as an essential resource for anyone looking to hone their analytical skills.

4. "The Art of Thinking Clearly" by Rolf Dobelli

Rolf Dobelli's "The Art of Thinking Clearly" presents a collection of cognitive biases and logical fallacies that often cloud our judgment. Each chapter focuses on a specific bias, illustrating how it manifests in daily life and decision-making. Dobelli's engaging prose and relatable examples provide readers with practical tools to recognize and counteract these mental shortcuts. This book serves as a vital reminder of the pitfalls of flawed reasoning, encouraging a more critical approach to our thoughts and beliefs.

5. "Superforecasting: The Art and Science of Prediction" by Philip E. Tetlock and Dan Gardner

In "Superforecasting," Philip Tetlock and Dan Gardner delve into the art of prediction, analyzing what distinguishes exceptional forecasters from their peers. The authors highlight the importance of analytical thinking, open-mindedness, and a willingness to revise one's beliefs in light of new evidence. Through compelling case studies and practical insights, they illustrate how critical thinking can enhance our ability to make accurate predictions about the future. This book not only emphasizes the value of rigorous thought but also showcases how such skills can lead to better decision-making in uncertain environments.

6. "The Elements of Reasoning" by Ronald Munson and Andrew Black

This concise guide provides readers with a foundational understanding of logical reasoning and argumentation. Munson and Black emphasize the importance of constructing and evaluating arguments effectively, providing clear explanations of concepts such as premises, conclusions, and fallacies. Through practical examples and exercises, they empower readers to engage critically with various forms of discourse, from everyday conversations to academic debates. This book is an invaluable resource for anyone looking to sharpen their analytical skills and engage more thoughtfully with the ideas presented by others.

7. "The Critical Thinking Toolkit" by Dr. David K. Lee

Dr. David K. Lee's "The Critical Thinking Toolkit" serves as a comprehensive guide for developing critical thinking skills across various contexts. It combines theoretical insights with practical exercises, encouraging readers to apply critical thinking in real-life situations. Lee's emphasis on problem-solving, decision-making, and reflective thinking equips readers with a robust framework for analyzing complex issues. This toolkit is particularly useful for students and professionals alike, fostering a culture of inquiry and thoughtful engagement in diverse fields.

8. "A More Beautiful Question: The Power of Inquiry to Spark Breakthrough Ideas" by Warren Berger

Warren Berger's "A More Beautiful Question" explores the transformative power of asking the right questions. He argues that inquiry is at the heart of innovation and creativity, and he encourages readers to cultivate a questioning mindset. Through a blend of storytelling and research, Berger illustrates how the best thinkers and innovators harness the power of inquiry to challenge the status quo and drive change. This book not only promotes critical thinking but also highlights the importance of curiosity as a catalyst for growth and discovery.

9. "Mindset: The New Psychology of Success" by Carol S. Dweck

In "Mindset," psychologist Carol Dweck introduces the concept of the growth mindset—the belief that abilities and intelligence can be developed through effort and learning. This perspective encourages individuals to embrace challenges, learn from failures, and persist in the face of obstacles. Dweck's insights foster critical thinking by promoting resilience and adaptability in one's approach to learning and problem-solving. Her work has significant implications for education and personal development, inspiring readers to adopt a more open and exploratory attitude toward their capabilities.

The promotion of critical thinking is a vital endeavor that enhances our ability to navigate an increasingly complex world. The aforementioned books not only illuminate the principles of critical thought but also inspire readers to engage deeply with ideas, challenge assumptions, and approach problems with an analytical mindset. By incorporating the insights from these works into our daily lives, we can cultivate a more thoughtful and reasoned approach to the myriad challenges we encounter, ultimately leading to more informed decisions and a richer understanding of the world around us. Embracing critical thinking is not just a personal journey; it is a collective imperative for fostering a more enlightened and rational society.

Part III:

Discipline and Reasoning

In the quiet chambers of the mind, where thoughts weave intricate patterns and ideas dance like shadows in the twilight, the twin pillars of discipline and reasoning stand resolute. They form the foundation of not only individual achievement but also the very architecture of civilization itself. Throughout history, great thinkers have revered these qualities, recognizing that they are not merely virtues to be aspired to, but essential tools for navigating the complexities of existence. As we embark on this exploration, we shall delve into the nature of discipline and reasoning, illuminating their profound interconnections and unveiling the mysteries that bind them.

Discipline, often perceived as a rigid framework, transcends mere adherence to rules; it is the art of cultivating focus and resilience. Like a masterful painter honing their craft, discipline allows the mind to refine its abilities and channel its energies towards meaningful pursuits. It requires an understanding of one's own limitations and the ability to transcend them, an endeavor fraught with challenges yet imbued with the potential for transformation. When practiced diligently, discipline transforms the chaotic orchestra of thoughts into a harmonious symphony, enabling the individual to navigate the labyrinth of life with clarity and purpose.

Conversely, reasoning serves as the compass in this intricate journey. It is the lens through which we perceive reality, a method of inquiry that leads us beyond the surface of appearances into the depths of understanding. Reasoning, like a finely crafted tool, allows us to dissect the complexities of the world, distinguishing between the ephemeral and the eternal. It empowers us to question assumptions, to seek evidence, and to construct coherent arguments, forging connections between disparate ideas. In this dance of logic and intuition, we discover that reasoning is not merely an academic exercise, but a pathway to wisdom.

The synergy between discipline and reasoning creates a fertile ground for intellectual growth and self-discovery. When cultivated together, they illuminate the pathways of creativity, innovation, and ethical decision-making. Discipline anchors our reasoning, providing the structure necessary to explore the depths of thought without drifting aimlessly. In turn, reasoning enriches our discipline, infusing it with purpose and insight. This dynamic interplay is not only vital for personal development but is also essential for the flourishing of societies that seek to engage thoughtfully with the myriad challenges of the contemporary world.

As we embark on this philosophical odyssey, it becomes clear that understanding how to develop discipline and reasoning is of paramount importance. Ancient philosophies, from Stoicism to Confucianism, have provided timeless insights into the cultivation of these virtues, while modern scientific research has unveiled the cognitive mechanisms underlying them. Through disciplined practice and the application of reasoned thought, we can embark on a transformative journey toward mastery, not just of skills, but of ourselves. In the chapters that follow, we will explore these philosophies and research findings, illuminating pathways that lead to the harmonious integration of discipline and reasoning, guiding us towards a more profound understanding of the self and the world around us.

Reasoning

Developing reasoning skills is a multifaceted endeavour that has garnered significant attention in both educational and psychological research. As reasoning encompasses critical thinking, problem-solving, and the ability to make informed decisions, understanding its development through scientific inquiry is paramount. Here, we explore various approaches, supported by research, that can enhance reasoning abilities across different age groups and contexts.

Cognitive Training Programs

Cognitive training has emerged as a prominent area of research aimed at enhancing reasoning skills. A meta-analysis conducted by Sala et al. (2019) examined the efficacy of various cognitive training programs. The study found that targeted cognitive training, particularly programs that focus on reasoning and problem-solving tasks, can lead to significant improvements in fluid intelligence and reasoning abilities. The researchers noted that tasks involving logical reasoning, pattern recognition, and deductive reasoning were particularly effective. These findings suggest that structured cognitive training can foster an environment conducive to developing reasoning skills, particularly when the training is deliberate and sustained over time.

Developing structured cognitive reasoning at home can be a rewarding endeavour that enhances critical thinking and problem-solving skills. By creating an environment conducive to inquiry and reflection, you can foster these abilities in yourself and your family. Here are some practical strategies to achieve this.

Encourage Curiosity and Questions

At the heart of cognitive reasoning lies curiosity. Cultivate an atmosphere where questions are welcomed and explored. Encourage family members to ask "why" and "how," and engage in discussions that delve into their interests. Use everyday experiences—like cooking or gardening—as springboards for questions. For example, if you're cooking, ask, "Why do we need to preheat the oven?" This not only sparks curiosity but also provides opportunities to discuss concepts like heat transfer and chemical reactions.

Create Problem-Solving Challenges

Incorporating problem-solving activities into your routine can significantly enhance reasoning skills. Consider setting up puzzles, logic games, or brain teasers that require analytical thinking. Board games like chess or strategy-based games can be particularly effective, as they encourage players to think ahead and consider various outcomes. You might also introduce real-world problems for family discussions, like planning a budget for a trip or deciding on a home improvement project. Such challenges promote critical thinking and collaborative reasoning.

Establish a Reading Culture

Reading is a powerful tool for developing cognitive reasoning. Create a family reading time where everyone engages with books, articles, or even podcasts. Choose diverse materials that encourage analysis and critical thought—fiction that explores complex characters or non-fiction that presents challenging concepts. After reading, discuss the material together, asking open-ended questions that require reasoning and reflection. For example, "What motivations do you think influenced the character's decisions?" This encourages deeper engagement with the content and sharpens reasoning abilities.

Implement Reflective Practices

Incorporating reflective practices into your daily routine can enhance cognitive reasoning. Encourage family members to maintain journals where they reflect on their day, thoughts, and experiences. Prompt them to analyze decisions they made or challenges they faced, asking guiding questions like, "What could I have done differently?" or "What did I learn from this situation?" Reflection fosters metacognition—the awareness of one's own thought processes—thereby enhancing reasoning skills over time.

Foster Open Discussions

Family discussions about various topics, from current events to ethical dilemmas, can serve as excellent exercises in reasoning. Choose subjects that are relevant and engaging for everyone involved. Encourage respectful debate and the expression of differing opinions. When engaging in discussions, model effective reasoning by articulating your thought process clearly. Ask others to explain their reasoning as well, which promotes a deeper understanding of how different perspectives can lead to varied conclusions.

Utilize Technology Wisely

Incorporating technology can also aid in developing cognitive reasoning skills. Educational apps and online resources focused on logic, mathematics, or science can provide interactive ways to enhance reasoning. Look for programs that offer challenges and track progress, allowing for both individual and family engagement. Additionally, consider using online forums or platforms for discussions on various topics, exposing family members to diverse viewpoints and encouraging critical analysis.

By fostering an environment rich in curiosity, problem-solving, reflective practices, and open dialogue, you can effectively develop structured cognitive reasoning at home. These strategies not only enhance individual skills but also strengthen family bonds, promoting a culture of inquiry and understanding that benefits everyone involved.

Educational Approaches

In educational settings, the integration of reasoning-focused curricula has proven beneficial. A study by Mercer and Sams (2006) investigated the impact of dialogic teaching on reasoning skills among primary school students. The researchers implemented teaching methods that encouraged students to engage in dialogue, collaboratively reasoning through problems and discussing their thought processes. The results indicated that students who participated in such interactive discussions demonstrated enhanced reasoning skills compared to those in traditional lecture-based environments. This highlights the importance of creating educational contexts that promote active engagement and critical discourse, fostering reasoning through social interaction.

The Role of Metacognition

Metacognition, or the awareness and understanding of one's own thought processes, plays a crucial role in developing reasoning abilities. Research by Schneider and Pressley (1997) underscores the significance of teaching metacognitive strategies to enhance reasoning. Their findings suggest that when individuals are trained to reflect on their reasoning processes—evaluating the strategies they use and considering alternative approaches—they become more adept at reasoning tasks. Techniques such as self-explanation, where learners articulate their thought processes aloud, have been shown to improve reasoning by encouraging deeper understanding and greater retention of information.

Critical Thinking Skills

Critical thinking, often viewed as synonymous with reasoning, is another area of research that provides insights into developing reasoning abilities. A study by Facione (2011) explored the impact of critical thinking instruction on reasoning skills in higher education. The findings revealed that courses specifically designed to teach critical thinking strategies, such as argument analysis and evidence evaluation, significantly improved students' reasoning capabilities. These results emphasize that critical thinking training is not only beneficial but essential for fostering higher-order reasoning skills, suggesting that educators should prioritize such curricula.

Collaborative Learning Environments

Collaborative learning environments have also been shown to enhance reasoning skills. A study by Johnson et al. (2014) investigated the effects of collaborative learning on the reasoning abilities of students in STEM fields. The researchers found that students who engaged in cooperative problem-solving tasks demonstrated improved reasoning skills compared to those who worked independently. The collaborative approach facilitated peer feedback, diverse perspectives, and collective problem-solving, which enriched students' reasoning processes. This suggests that fostering collaborative learning environments can be a powerful strategy for enhancing reasoning.

Mindfulness and Reasoning

Recent studies have also examined the impact of mindfulness on reasoning abilities. Research by Zeidan et al. (2010) indicated that mindfulness meditation can lead to improvements in cognitive flexibility and executive functioning, both of which are critical components of effective reasoning. Participants who engaged in mindfulness practices demonstrated enhanced attention and the ability to consider multiple perspectives when reasoning through complex problems. This highlights the potential of mindfulness training as a tool for developing reasoning skills by promoting a more focused and flexible cognitive state.

Feedback Mechanisms

The role of feedback in developing reasoning abilities cannot be understated. Research by Hattie and Timperley (2007) synthesized findings on the importance of feedback in educational contexts. The study concluded that effective feedback, particularly when it is specific, timely, and constructive, significantly enhances learning outcomes, including reasoning skills. Providing learners with opportunities to receive feedback on their reasoning processes—through peer reviews, instructor comments, or self-assessments—can lead to deeper understanding and refinement of their reasoning abilities.

Technology and Reasoning Development

In our increasingly digital age, technology-based interventions have also been explored for their effectiveness in developing reasoning skills. A study by Clarke-Midura and Popp (2014) examined the use of digital simulations in teaching complex problem-solving and reasoning skills. The researchers found that engaging with interactive simulations allowed students to experiment with different scenarios, fostering a deeper understanding of causal relationships and enhancing their reasoning capabilities. This indicates that technology can serve as a valuable adjunct to traditional teaching methods, providing dynamic and engaging ways to develop reasoning skills.

In conclusion, the development of reasoning skills is supported by a rich body of scientific research that spans cognitive training, educational approaches, metacognitive strategies, collaborative learning, and the integration of technology. Each of these avenues provides valuable insights into how individuals can enhance their reasoning abilities, whether through structured training programs, engaging educational environments, or reflective practices. As we continue to explore the complexities of human cognition, it becomes increasingly clear that fostering reasoning is not merely an academic pursuit; it is essential for navigating the intricate tapestry of life, making informed decisions, and engaging thoughtfully with the world. The integration of these findings into educational practices and personal development strategies can pave the way for a more reasoned and reflective society, equipped to tackle the challenges of the future.

Developing Reasoning in a Philosophical Conduct

In the vast ground of human thought, reasoning stands as a shimmering thread, weaving together the disparate elements of knowledge, experience, and inquiry. To develop reasoning is to embark on a philosophical journey, one that invites us to ponder the very nature of understanding itself. This quest, both personal and collective, is underscored by the idea that reasoning is not merely a skill to be honed but a profound practice of engaging with the world and our place within it.

To begin this exploration, we must first consider the roots of reasoning in the philosophical tradition. From Socrates, who championed the dialectical method, to Kant, who sought to delineate the boundaries of human understanding, thinkers have long recognized reasoning as the cornerstone of wisdom. It is through reason that we navigate the complexities of existence, distinguishing between mere opinion and knowledge. Thus, developing reasoning is akin to polishing a mirror, enabling us to reflect more clearly upon our beliefs, biases, and the intricate patterns of thought that govern our lives.

At its essence, reasoning invites us to engage in a dance of ideas, a graceful interplay between assertion and inquiry. To cultivate this skill, we must nurture a mindset steeped in curiosity and openness. Philosophers such as John Dewey emphasized the importance of reflective thought in fostering genuine understanding. This reflection is not a passive act; it is an active engagement with our experiences and the questions they raise. By embracing uncertainty and allowing ourselves to wonder, we create fertile ground for the seeds of reasoning to take root.

As we delve deeper into this process, we encounter the notion of dialogue—an essential companion to reasoning. In the tradition of Plato's dialogues, the exchange of ideas is presented as a transformative experience. Through dialogue, we not only articulate our thoughts but also invite others to challenge and refine them. This engagement creates a dynamic environment where reasoning flourishes, unearthing insights that might remain buried in solitary contemplation. The act of articulating one's thoughts, of putting them into the crucible of discussion, can lead to unexpected revelations, illuminating the shadows that often cloud our understanding.

Moreover, embracing ambiguity is vital in the journey toward refined reasoning. The philosopher Friedrich Nietzsche posited that confronting the chaos of existence can lead to a richer understanding of life. Reasoning, then, is not about imposing rigid structures upon our thoughts but about embracing the fluidity of ideas. When we learn to navigate the grey areas—where questions often outweigh answers—we become adept at employing reasoning as a tool for exploration rather than an instrument of certainty. This philosophical stance encourages a humble approach to knowledge, where we acknowledge the limits of our understanding while remaining open to the infinite possibilities that lie beyond.

The development of reasoning also requires a commitment to introspection. The practice of self-examination, advocated by thinkers like Descartes, enables us to peel back the layers of our assumptions and beliefs. It is a form of philosophical alchemy, transforming the raw material of our experiences into the gold of insight. By regularly engaging in reflective practices—be it through journaling, meditation, or contemplation—we cultivate a deeper awareness of our thought processes. This self-awareness, in turn, sharpens our reasoning, allowing us to discern the influences that shape our judgments and decisions.

Furthermore, engaging with the great works of philosophy can serve as both inspiration and challenge in the pursuit of reasoning. The texts of ancient and contemporary philosophers offer a rich reservoir of ideas, each inviting us to grapple with profound questions. By immersing ourselves in the dialectics of thought presented by figures like Aristotle, Hume, or Arendt, we not only expand our intellectual horizons but also confront the complexities of reasoning itself. Engaging critically with these works encourages us to dissect arguments, analyze assumptions, and construct our own reasoned perspectives.

In this labyrinth of thought, we must also acknowledge the role of ethics in reasoning. The philosopher Immanuel Kant asserted that reason is not merely a tool for understanding the world but a means of engaging with moral imperatives. Developing reasoning, therefore, is inextricably linked to cultivating ethical awareness. As we refine our ability to think critically, we must also consider the implications of our reasoning on ourselves and others. This ethical dimension invites us to ask: How does our reasoning impact our choices? Are we using our reasoning to promote understanding and compassion, or are we wielding it as a weapon to justify prejudice and division?

As we navigate the realms of reasoning, the integration of diverse perspectives emerges as a crucial aspect of development. Engaging with ideas and experiences that challenge our own allows us to expand the boundaries of our reasoning. This interplay of perspectives fosters a richer, more nuanced understanding of the world. Philosophers like Martha Nussbaum advocate for a global citizenship that recognizes our interconnectedness. In this spirit, embracing diverse viewpoints not only enhances our reasoning but also fosters empathy—a vital quality in an increasingly polarized world.

Ultimately, the journey toward developing reasoning is a lifelong endeavor, one that intertwines the personal with the philosophical. It calls for patience, humility, and an unwavering commitment to inquiry.

The paths we traverse may be winding, filled with moments of doubt and uncertainty, but they are also rich with opportunities for growth and enlightenment. As we embrace the complexities of reasoning, we come to appreciate it as a journey rather than a destination—an ever-evolving dance with the mysteries of existence.

In conclusion, developing reasoning is not solely about enhancing intellectual capabilities; it is an invitation to engage with the profound questions that define our humanity. Through curiosity, dialogue, introspection, and ethical awareness, we can cultivate a reasoning practice that enriches our lives and deepens our understanding of the world. As we embark on this philosophical journey, let us remain open to the mysteries that await, for in the dance of reasoning lies the potential for transformative insight and profound connection.

Discipline is often heralded as the cornerstone of personal growth and achievement, a principle deeply embedded in the teachings of ancient philosophers and warriors alike. The importance of discipline transcends cultures and epochs, manifesting in various ways as a means of achieving excellence, fostering resilience, and cultivating virtue. By examining the lives and philosophies of figures such as Socrates, Marcus Aurelius, Arjuna, and Karna, we can uncover the profound significance of discipline in shaping character and guiding actions.

The Philosophical Underpinnings of Discipline

Socrates, one of the most influential figures in Western philosophy, exemplified the power of discipline in the pursuit of knowledge and virtue. His method of dialectical questioning—often referred to as the Socratic Method—required a disciplined mind, one capable of critical reflection and rigorous self-examination. Socrates believed that an unexamined life was not worth living, emphasizing the need for individuals to cultivate discipline in their thoughts and actions. This discipline was not merely about adhering to rules; it was about striving for a deeper understanding of oneself and the world.

In this light, discipline becomes an internal compass, guiding individuals through the tumult of life. For Socrates, the ability to question and reflect was a form of self-discipline that paved the way for genuine insight and wisdom. His eventual martyrdom for his beliefs underscores the ultimate sacrifice that discipline may demand: the commitment to truth, even in the face of adversity. Socrates teaches us that discipline is the foundation upon which a meaningful life is constructed, as it allows us to remain steadfast in our pursuit of virtue, despite external pressures.

The Stoic Perspective

Turning to Marcus Aurelius, the Roman emperor and Stoic philosopher, we find a robust articulation of discipline as an essential element of personal integrity and leadership. His meditations offer a glimpse into the disciplined mind of a ruler who faced numerous challenges, from military conflicts to personal loss. Aurelius believed that discipline was crucial for maintaining inner tranquility amidst external chaos. He wrote about the importance of self-control, urging individuals to master their impulses and desires in order to align their actions with their principles.

For Marcus Aurelius, discipline was not just a means to personal well-being but a pathway to effective leadership. A disciplined leader can inspire others, instilling a sense of purpose and order within their community. His reflections remind us that discipline is a form of service—both to oneself and to others. By practising self-discipline, we cultivate resilience and strength, enabling us to face challenges with equanimity. In this sense, discipline is a vital tool for navigating the complexities of life, allowing us to act with intention rather than reaction.

The Warrior's Discipline

In the realm of epic narratives, the figures of Arjuna and Karna from the Indian epic, the Mahabharata, serve as powerful examples of discipline in the context of duty and moral dilemmas. Arjuna, a skilled archer and warrior, grapples with profound inner conflict on the battlefield of Kurukshetra. Faced with the moral implications of fighting against his kin, Arjuna initially falters, overwhelmed by doubt and despair. However, under the guidance of Lord Krishna, he learns that discipline is essential not only in martial skills but also in understanding one's duty (dharma).

Krishna emphasizes that true discipline involves aligning one's actions with higher principles, and transcending personal attachments and emotions. This disciplined approach allows Arjuna to rise above his turmoil, fulfilling his responsibilities as a warrior and protector. His journey illustrates that discipline is not merely about rigid adherence to rules; it is a dynamic process of self-discovery and ethical commitment. By embracing his duty, Arjuna exemplifies the transformative power of discipline, enabling him to act in accordance with his values even in the face of tremendous adversity.

In contrast, Karna presents a complex narrative about discipline shaped by loyalty and personal honour. As a warrior of great skill and valour, Karna remains fiercely loyal to his friend Duryodhana, even when faced with moral ambiguity. His discipline is evident in his unwavering commitment to his friend, which, while admirable, also leads him into conflict with his own values. Karna's story highlights a dual aspect of discipline: it can serve as a guiding light, but it can also become a source of conflict when loyalty and duty are misaligned with ethical considerations.

Karna's tragic fate prompts reflection on the importance of discerning which principles we choose to uphold. Discipline must be coupled with wisdom to ensure that our commitments align with a broader understanding of virtue and justice. In this context, the discipline of thought becomes paramount, reminding us that true strength lies not only in adherence to one's word but in the ability to evaluate the moral implications of our choices.

The Contemporary Relevance of Discipline

The lessons gleaned from Socrates, Marcus Aurelius, Arjuna, and Karna resonate powerfully in our modern context. In a world filled with distractions and competing demands, the ability to cultivate discipline can profoundly impact personal growth and fulfilment. Whether in the realm of academics, professional pursuits, or personal relationships, discipline remains a vital ingredient for success.

Discipline nurtures resilience, allowing individuals to persist in the face of challenges. It cultivates a mindset that values effort and commitment over immediate gratification. This principle echoes the Stoic philosophy espoused by Marcus Aurelius, reminding us that true freedom lies in our capacity to choose our responses to external circumstances. By embracing discipline, we can cultivate a sense of agency that empowers us to navigate life's trials with grace and integrity.

Moreover, in an age of rapid change and uncertainty, the philosophical reflections of ancient thinkers encourage us to engage in self-examination and reflection. Much like Socrates' call for an examined life, we are urged to question our beliefs, motivations, and actions. By doing so, we foster a disciplined mind capable of making informed and ethical choices. This commitment to self-awareness and accountability allows us to remain aligned with our values, even when faced with the complexities of modern existence.

In summation, the importance of discipline is woven throughout the fabric of human history, exemplified by the lives of Socrates, Marcus Aurelius, Arjuna, and Karna. Each figure illuminates different facets of discipline—its role in the pursuit of knowledge, ethical leadership, duty, and personal honour. As we reflect on their teachings, we are reminded that discipline is not merely a tool for achievement; it is a profound practice of self-cultivation that shapes our character and guides our actions.

In embracing discipline, we open ourselves to a life of purpose and integrity, fostering resilience in the face of adversity. As we navigate our own journeys, let us carry forth the wisdom of these ancient thinkers, cultivating the discipline necessary to forge a meaningful existence and contribute positively to the world around us. Ultimately, discipline is a path toward mastery, self-discovery, and the realization of our fullest potential.

Discipline

Discipline is a quality revered across cultures and eras, often viewed as the bedrock of personal development and achievement. Whether through the lens of philosophy, literature, or historical example, the lessons surrounding discipline resonate with profound significance. Figures from ancient epics and philosophies—such as Arjuna and Karna from *The Mahabharata*, the Stoic thinkers, the intrepid Vikings, and the disciplined Spartans—provide us with invaluable insights into the cultivation of unbreakable discipline. This essay delves into the principles of discipline, drawing from these rich narratives to offer practical strategies for developing this essential trait.

Defining Purpose

The journey toward unbreakable discipline begins with a clear understanding of one's purpose. In *The Mahabharata*, Arjuna's transformation from a conflicted warrior to a decisive fighter exemplifies this principle. Initially, he is overwhelmed by doubt as he faces the moral implications of battling his own kin. However, guided by Lord Krishna, he comes to realize the importance of his dharma—his duty as a warrior. This pivotal moment illuminates a key point: discipline is anchored in a profound sense of purpose.

To cultivate unbreakable discipline, begin by asking yourself what drives you. Define your long-term goals, aspirations, and the values that underpin them. This purpose serves as a compass, directing your actions and providing motivation even in the face of adversity. The clarity of purpose will empower you to stay disciplined, especially when challenges arise. As Arjuna ultimately learns, aligning your actions with your purpose is a powerful catalyst for unwavering commitment.

Embracing Training and Preparation

The Spartans epitomized the essence of rigorous training and preparation. From a young age, Spartan boys were enrolled in the agoge, an intense educational and training program designed to instill discipline, physical fitness, and mental toughness. This system was not merely about preparing for battle; it was about forging character, resilience, and loyalty to their community.

To cultivate your own discipline, establish a consistent routine that incorporates various forms of training. This could involve physical exercise, skill development, or intellectual pursuits. Like the Spartans, prioritize preparation and practice, as discipline is cultivated through repetition and commitment. Whether it's a daily workout, dedicated study hours, or honing a craft, regular engagement fosters habits that become second nature. This foundational discipline reinforces your ability to meet your goals with determination and tenacity.

Practicing Self-Control

The Stoic philosophers, such as Epictetus and Marcus Aurelius, emphasized the vital role of self-control in developing discipline. Marcus Aurelius, in his *Meditations*, reflects on the necessity of mastering one's impulses and desires to maintain inner tranquility. The Stoics believed that true strength lies in the ability to govern oneself, rather than being governed by external circumstances.

To develop unbreakable discipline, practice self-control in your daily life. This might mean resisting distractions, setting firm boundaries, or refraining from immediate gratification. In a world rife with temptations, cultivating self-control is crucial. Start by identifying areas where you struggle to maintain discipline and implement small changes to reinforce your resolve. For instance, if you find it challenging to focus on work, establish specific time blocks for concentrated effort, free from interruptions.

Self-control can also be exercised through mindfulness practices, allowing you to develop greater awareness of your impulses and responses. By recognizing triggers that lead to distraction or indulgence, you can make conscious choices that align with your long-term goals. The Stoics remind us that the path to true freedom lies in our ability to choose our responses to life's challenges, and this choice is a product of disciplined self-control.

Creating a Supportive Environment

The Vikings exemplified the importance of camaraderie and loyalty in fostering discipline. Their culture was characterized by strong bonds among clan members, who supported one another through both conquests and everyday challenges. This sense of community was integral to their success, as it encouraged individual discipline through shared values and mutual accountability.

To forge unbreakable discipline, surround yourself with like-minded individuals who encourage your growth. This support system can be instrumental in maintaining motivation and accountability. Seek out communities, whether in person or online, that share your aspirations and values. Engage with mentors who can guide you and peers who can inspire you to stay committed to your goals.

Additionally, consider how your environment influences your discipline. Create a space that fosters focus and productivity. Declutter distractions and design an area conducive to your pursuits—be it a study nook for learning, a workout space for physical training, or a quiet corner for reflection. By curating your environment thoughtfully, you reinforce the habits and behaviors that align with your disciplined mindset.

Embracing Challenges as Opportunities

The epic tales of *The Mahabharata* reveal the profound significance of embracing challenges as opportunities for growth. Arjuna's journey on the battlefield illustrates this principle, as he faces immense inner conflict. Through Krishna's guidance, he learns to view his challenges not as burdens, but as essential aspects of his path toward self-actualization.

Karna, too, embodies this notion. Despite facing societal stigma and personal adversity, he remains committed to his training and loyalty to Duryodhana. His discipline allows him to navigate his challenges with grace and determination. The lessons from both Arjuna and Karna highlight that challenges are intrinsic to the human experience, and how we respond to them shapes our character and discipline.

To develop unbreakable discipline, cultivate a mindset that views challenges as opportunities for growth. When obstacles arise, instead of succumbing to frustration, ask yourself what you can learn from the experience. This proactive approach not only strengthens your resolve but also reinforces your commitment to your goals. Each challenge overcome is a testament to your discipline, serving as a building block for future endeavors.

Reflecting and Adapting

The Stoics advocated for regular self-reflection as a means of fostering resilience and discipline. Marcus Aurelius's practice of journaling and self-examination allowed him to assess his thoughts and actions critically. This reflective practice reinforces the idea that discipline is not a static quality; it requires ongoing assessment and adaptation.

Set aside time for regular introspection to develop unbreakable discipline. Analyze your progress, identify areas for improvement, and adjust your strategies accordingly. Reflecting on your experiences enables you to recognize patterns in your behavior and helps you adapt your approach as needed. This ongoing reflection ensures that your discipline evolves in alignment with your goals and values.

Moreover, seek feedback from trusted peers or mentors. Constructive criticism can provide insights that you may overlook on your own, further refining your approach to discipline. The Stoic practice of reflection allows you to remain humble and open to growth, which is essential for maintaining unbreakable discipline over time.

Setting Clear Boundaries

The disciplined lifestyle of the Spartans was governed by strict codes of conduct and expectations. They adhered to a well-defined structure that emphasized duty, loyalty, and excellence. This disciplined way of life not only shaped their character but also fostered a sense of community and purpose.

To forge unbreakable discipline, establish clear boundaries for yourself regarding work, leisure, and commitments. Identify your priorities and create a structured schedule that aligns with your goals. Setting boundaries can help you minimize distractions and maintain focus on what truly matters. This could involve designating specific times for study, work, or physical training, while also allowing for adequate rest and recovery.

Additionally, learn to say no to commitments that do not align with your goals or values. The ability to set boundaries is a critical aspect of discipline, allowing you to protect your time and energy for pursuits that matter most. By adhering to a structured lifestyle, you reinforce your commitment to discipline, making it easier to navigate life's demands.

Cultivating Mental Toughness

Viking culture celebrated bravery, resilience, and mental toughness. Their legendary expeditions and battles often demanded extraordinary fortitude and discipline. To cultivate unbreakable discipline, develop your mental toughness through practices that challenge your comfort zones.

Engage in activities that push your limits, whether physically or mentally. This could include endurance training, public speaking, or tackling difficult subjects. By willingly facing challenges, you strengthen your resolve and build confidence in your ability to overcome obstacles. Mental toughness is a crucial component of discipline, as it allows you to stay committed to your goals even when faced with discomfort or adversity.

Furthermore, consider incorporating mindfulness practices, such as meditation or visualization, into your routine. These techniques can help you build resilience by enhancing your awareness of thoughts and emotions, enabling you to respond to challenges with clarity and focus. As you cultivate mental toughness, you'll find that your discipline becomes increasingly unshakeable.

Celebrating Small Wins

The narratives of *The Mahabharata* and Viking lore highlight the importance of acknowledging victories, no matter how small. Celebrating progress helps reinforce discipline by fostering a sense of achievement and motivation. Arjuna's growth throughout the epic serves as a reminder that each step forward contributes to the larger journey.

To develop unbreakable discipline, set smaller milestones along the way to achieving your larger goals. Celebrate these milestones with intention, whether through reflection, rewards, or sharing your achievements with supportive peers. This practice not only boosts motivation but also reinforces a positive mindset that sustains your commitment to discipline.

Recognizing small wins fosters resilience by reminding you that progress is a cumulative process. When you acknowledge your achievements, you reinforce the belief that discipline yields results, encouraging you to persist in your efforts. Each small victory serves as a stepping stone on your path to success.

Committing to Lifelong Learning

The Stoics believed in the value of continuous self-improvement. Engaging in lifelong learning enriches your mind and fortifies your discipline. Whether through reading, attending workshops, or seeking mentorship, committing to expanding your knowledge and skills is crucial for personal growth.

Books have long been revered as vessels of knowledge, wisdom, and insight, serving as essential tools in the cultivation of discipline. They offer not just information, but pathways to introspection, self-improvement, and a deeper understanding of our potential. Engaging with literature can significantly enhance our ability to forge unbreakable discipline in several profound ways.

Books invite us into the minds of others, allowing us to see the world through different lenses. This exploration fosters self-reflection, an essential component of discipline. Through the characters we encounter and the dilemmas they face, we are prompted to examine our own values, behaviours, and motivations. For instance, reading about figures like Marcus Aurelius or Viktor Frankl can inspire us to confront our own challenges with resilience and purpose. This reflection helps us identify areas where we need to cultivate greater discipline, aligning our actions with our core beliefs.

Engaging with a book requires focus and commitment, encouraging us to cultivate a disciplined approach to our time. In an age of constant distraction, dedicating time to read fosters a habit of intentionality. Setting aside specific times for reading creates a structured routine, reinforcing the idea that discipline involves prioritizing our goals over fleeting distractions. This act of carving out quiet moments for contemplation not only enhances our understanding but also trains our minds to concentrate and delve deeply into a subject.

Books provide access to the wisdom of those who have traversed the paths of discipline before us. Biographies, autobiographies, and philosophical texts offer insights into the lives of individuals who exemplified discipline in their pursuits. By studying their journeys—be it a warrior like Arjuna in *The Mahabharata*, a philosopher like Epictetus, or a leader like Nelson Mandela—we can glean valuable lessons about perseverance, commitment, and the importance of maintaining focus amid adversity. These narratives serve as blueprints, guiding us as we strive to emulate their disciplined approaches to life.

Reading fosters a growth mindset, the belief that our abilities and intelligence can be developed through dedication and hard work. Books that focus on self-improvement, resilience, and personal development encourage us to embrace challenges as opportunities for growth. This perspective is integral to forging discipline; when we view obstacles as stepping stones rather than barriers, we become more willing to engage in the sustained effort required to achieve our goals. The insights gained from literature can help us reframe our mindset, enabling us to persist in our endeavours with renewed vigour.

In the pages of a book, we often find frameworks for goal-setting and accountability. Many self-help and productivity books provide actionable strategies that can help us design our own discipline frameworks. Techniques such as habit tracking, journaling, and creating structured plans can be drawn from these texts, allowing us to hold ourselves accountable. By implementing the lessons learned from literature, we take concrete steps toward developing the discipline necessary to achieve our aspirations.

In essence, books are not merely repositories of knowledge; they are transformative tools that can profoundly shape our capacity for discipline. Through reflection, structured engagement, inspiration from exemplary lives, and the cultivation of a growth mindset, literature empowers us to forge a disciplined path toward our goals. As we immerse ourselves in the written word, we discover that the journey of discipline is not a solitary one; it is enriched by the wisdom of those who have come before us, guiding us toward our fullest potential.

Again, here are some books which provide great insights into building discipline:

1. "Atomic Habits" by James Clear

Overview: In *Atomic Habits*, James Clear presents a comprehensive framework for understanding how habits work and how they can be changed. He emphasizes the idea that small changes can lead to remarkable results over time. Clear breaks down the mechanics of habit formation and provides actionable strategies for building positive habits while breaking negative ones.

Key Takeaways:

- **The 1% Rule:** Clear argues that improving just 1% every day leads to significant growth over time. Discipline is cultivated by focusing on small, manageable changes rather than overwhelming transformations.
- **Cue, Craving, Response, Reward:** Understanding this habit loop is essential for modifying behaviors. By identifying cues and

crafting responses, individuals can design their environments to promote discipline.
- **Identity-Based Habits:** Shift your focus from what you want to achieve to who you wish to become. This identity-centric approach helps reinforce discipline by aligning your habits with your self-image.

2. "The Power of Habit" by Charles Duhigg

Overview: Charles Duhigg's *The Power of Habit* delves into the science of habit formation and how understanding our habits can lead to personal and professional success. Duhigg introduces the concept of the habit loop—cue, routine, reward—and provides insights into how to harness this knowledge for better discipline.

Key Takeaways:

- **Habit Loop:** By breaking down habits into their components, readers can identify areas for change and implement new routines that lead to healthier behaviors.
- **Keystone Habits:** Certain habits have the power to trigger a chain reaction of positive changes. By focusing on keystone habits, individuals can cultivate discipline that spills over into other areas of their lives.
- **Willpower as a Muscle:** Duhigg describes willpower as a finite resource that can be strengthened through practice, much like a

muscle. Developing discipline requires consistent exercise of willpower in daily choices.

3. "The 7 Habits of Highly Effective People" by Stephen R. Covey

Overview: Stephen Covey's classic, *The 7 Habits of Highly Effective People*, offers a holistic approach to personal and professional effectiveness. Covey emphasizes principles and character ethics over mere techniques, presenting habits that foster discipline and integrity.

Key Takeaways:

- **Be Proactive:** Taking responsibility for your actions is the foundation of discipline. Covey encourages readers to recognize that they have the power to choose their responses to any situation.
- **Begin with the End in Mind:** Establishing clear goals and a vision for your life fosters direction and purpose, crucial for maintaining discipline in the face of challenges.
- **Put First Things First:** Prioritization is key to effective discipline. By focusing on what matters most and managing time effectively, individuals can cultivate a disciplined approach to their commitments.

4. "Discipline Equals Freedom: Field Manual" by Jocko Willink

Overview: Former Navy SEAL Jocko Willink's *Discipline Equals Freedom* is a motivational guide that emphasizes the correlation between discipline and personal freedom. Willink shares his insights from military training to provide a no-nonsense approach to cultivating discipline in everyday life.

Key Takeaways:

- **The Dichotomy of Discipline:** Willink argues that while discipline may seem restrictive, it ultimately leads to greater freedom. By establishing discipline, individuals can break free from the constraints of bad habits and procrastination.
- **Extreme Ownership:** Taking full responsibility for one's life and choices is crucial for building discipline. This mindset fosters accountability and encourages proactive behavior.
- **The Power of Routine:** Willink advocates for a structured daily routine that includes exercise, planning, and reflection. Consistency in these practices strengthens discipline over time.

5. "Mindset: The New Psychology of Success" by Carol S. Dweck

Overview: In *Mindset*, psychologist Carol Dweck explores the concept of fixed versus growth mindsets and how they influence our approach to challenges and learning. This book provides valuable insights into the psychological foundations of discipline.

Key Takeaways:

- **Embracing a Growth Mindset:** Adopting a growth mindset encourages resilience and perseverance, essential traits for building discipline. This perspective allows individuals to view failures as opportunities for learning.
- **The Role of Effort:** Dweck emphasizes that effort is a key component of success. Understanding that discipline requires sustained effort can help individuals remain committed to their goals.
- **Feedback and Adaptation:** A growth mindset involves being open to feedback and willing to adapt strategies based on experiences. This flexibility is crucial for maintaining discipline through challenges.

6. "Grit: The Power of Passion and Perseverance" by Angela Duckworth

Overview: Angela Duckworth's *Grit* examines the role of passion and perseverance in achieving long-term goals. Duckworth posits that talent alone is not enough; discipline and sustained effort are vital for success.

Key Takeaways:

- **The Importance of Grit:** Duckworth defines grit as a combination of passion and perseverance. Cultivating grit requires consistent effort over time, reinforcing the idea that discipline is essential for achieving meaningful goals.
- **Cultivating Interest:** Finding and nurturing genuine interests can enhance motivation and commitment. When individuals are passionate about their pursuits, discipline becomes less of a chore and more of a rewarding practice.
- **Practice and Mastery:** Duckworth emphasizes the value of deliberate practice in developing expertise. A disciplined approach to honing skills is crucial for achieving mastery in any field.

7. "The War of Art" by Steven Pressfield

Overview: In *The War of Art*, Steven Pressfield tackles the challenges of resistance that creatives face. He argues that discipline is the antidote to the resistance that often prevents individuals from pursuing their passions.

Key Takeaways:

- **Recognizing Resistance:** Pressfield identifies resistance as a force that manifests in various forms, often leading to procrastination and

self-doubt. Acknowledging this resistance is the first step toward overcoming it.
- **Turning Pro:** Pressfield distinguishes between amateurs and professionals. The latter adopt a disciplined mindset, committing to their craft regardless of external circumstances or internal struggles.
- **Daily Practice:** Establishing a routine that includes dedicated time for creative work fosters discipline. By showing up consistently, individuals can combat resistance and cultivate their craft.

8. "Can't Hurt Me: Master Your Mind and Defy the Odds" by David Goggins

Overview: In *Can't Hurt Me*, former Navy SEAL David Goggins shares his remarkable life story and the lessons he learned about mental toughness and discipline. Goggins' journey from a challenging childhood to becoming a decorated veteran exemplifies the power of relentless discipline.

Key Takeaways:

- **Embrace Discomfort:** Goggins argues that true growth occurs outside of our comfort zones. By willingly facing discomfort, individuals can develop mental resilience and discipline.
- **Accountability Mirror:** Goggins encourages readers to confront their shortcomings

honestly. This practice fosters self-awareness and helps individuals take ownership of their discipline.
- **The 40% Rule:** Goggins posits that most people only tap into 40% of their potential. Recognizing this can inspire individuals to push beyond perceived limits and cultivate unbreakable discipline.

9. "The Compound Effect" by Darren Hardy

Overview: Darren Hardy's *The Compound Effect* explores the power of small, consistent actions over time. Hardy emphasizes that discipline in everyday choices can lead to significant long-term results.

Key Takeaways:

- **Small Choices Matter:** Hardy illustrates how seemingly insignificant decisions compound over time, leading to either success or failure. This insight underscores the importance of discipline in daily life.
- **Tracking Progress:** Hardy advocates for tracking habits and behaviors to understand patterns. This practice helps reinforce discipline by highlighting areas for improvement.
- **Momentum:** By building small successes, individuals create momentum that fuels further discipline and achievement. Each step

forward reinforces the commitment to personal growth.

10. "Essentialism: The Disciplined Pursuit of Less" by Greg McKeown

Overview: In *Essentialism*, Greg McKeown argues for the importance of prioritization and focus in achieving meaningful results. He advocates for a disciplined approach to determining what truly matters.

Key Takeaways:

- **Focus on the Essential:** McKeown emphasizes the importance of identifying and concentrating on what truly matters. Discipline involves saying no to distractions and commitments that do not align with your goals.
- **The Power of Choice:** Understanding that you have the power to choose how you spend your time fosters a disciplined mindset. This awareness encourages intentionality in decision-making.
- **Buffer Time:** McKeown suggests incorporating buffer time into schedules to manage unexpected challenges. This proactive approach enhances discipline by allowing flexibility without derailing progress.

And now one of my favourite books of all time, Discipline is Destiny by Ryan Holiday.

Historical Context

One of the book's central themes is the examination of historical figures who exemplified unbreakable discipline. Holiday draws heavily from the life of Marcus Aurelius, the Roman Emperor and renowned Stoic philosopher. Aurelius's commitment to discipline is evident in his daily practices, which included reflection, journaling, and a steadfast focus on self-improvement. His famous work, *Meditations*, serves as a testament to the power of discipline in navigating the complexities of leadership and personal conduct. By documenting his thoughts, Aurelius not only cultivated self-awareness but also reinforced his commitment to Stoic principles, such as control over one's reactions and a dedication to virtue.

The Art of Journaling

Holiday emphasizes the transformative power of journaling as a tool for building discipline. He explains how Aurelius used journaling not merely as a means of reflection but as a way to hold himself accountable for his actions. This practice encourages individuals to confront their thoughts, decisions, and behaviors honestly. By writing down goals and reflecting on progress, one cultivates a disciplined mindset that can withstand the trials of life. The act of journaling itself becomes a disciplined ritual, fostering a deeper connection to one's aspirations and reinforcing the importance of consistency.

Establishing Routines

Another key aspect of the book is the focus on structured daily routines. Holiday posits that success is often built on consistent habits rather than fleeting moments of inspiration. He discusses how disciplined individuals, such as athletes and artists, establish routines that prioritize their goals and manage their time effectively. For instance, an athlete's commitment to training, regardless of external conditions, exemplifies the kind of discipline that leads to excellence. By encouraging readers to create their own frameworks for success—whether through morning rituals, exercise regimens, or focused work sessions—Holiday illustrates that discipline is a practice that can be cultivated over time.

Resilience in Adversity

The theme of resilience is interwoven throughout the narrative, as Holiday examines how discipline enables individuals to persevere through difficult times. He shares inspiring stories of people who faced immense challenges but remained committed to their principles and goals. For instance, he highlights the journey of individuals like Viktor Frankl, who, despite experiencing unimaginable suffering in concentration camps, maintained a disciplined mindset that focused on purpose and meaning. This resilience, rooted in discipline, reveals that enduring hardship can lead to personal growth and a profound understanding of one's values.

Mindfulness and Focus

In an age characterized by distractions, Holiday underscores the importance of mindfulness in cultivating discipline. He advocates for being present and focused on the task at hand, as this awareness enhances one's ability to resist temptations and distractions. Practicing mindfulness allows individuals to engage fully in their endeavors, whether they are pursuing a professional project or personal goal. By training the mind to focus, one can develop a disciplined approach that reinforces commitment and minimizes procrastination.

The Stoic Virtues

Holiday aligns discipline with the Stoic virtues of courage, justice, wisdom, and temperance. He discusses how these virtues interconnect with disciplined behavior, promoting a life of integrity and purpose. For instance, courage is not merely about facing fear; it is about consistently making the right choices even when it is difficult. By embodying these Stoic virtues, individuals can cultivate a disciplined mindset that guides their actions and decisions. The intersection of discipline and virtue forms a moral compass that can steer one through life's challenges.

Long-Term Vision

Another critical component of discipline discussed in the book is the development of a long-term vision. Holiday emphasizes that discipline is not merely about immediate gratification; it is about making choices that align with one's future aspirations. By keeping a long-term perspective, individuals are better equipped to stay disciplined in their daily efforts. For example, an aspiring writer might face numerous rejections, but if they maintain a vision of their future success and commitment to honing their craft, they are more likely to persevere through the setbacks. Each small action, taken with discipline, contributes to the larger goal of realizing that vision.

Accountability and Community

Holiday also highlights the importance of accountability in the journey toward discipline. He encourages readers to seek out communities or relationships that reinforce their commitments. Surrounding oneself with disciplined individuals fosters an environment where accountability thrives. For instance, joining a writing group or an exercise class can provide external motivation and support, making it easier to stay committed to one's goals. This sense of community can act as a catalyst for discipline, as individuals share their struggles and successes, inspiring one another to maintain focus.

Embracing Discomfort

A significant insight from *Discipline is Destiny* is the necessity of embracing discomfort. Holiday argues that true growth occurs outside of our comfort zones. By willingly facing challenges and discomfort, individuals can develop mental resilience and discipline. This idea is vividly illustrated through stories of athletes who push their limits, artists who expose themselves to criticism, and leaders who confront difficult decisions. By reframing discomfort as an opportunity for growth, one can cultivate the discipline necessary to tackle life's challenges head-on.

Chapter 3: Conversations with the Eternal

The Divine Alchemy

The connection between humanity and the divine serves as a profound cornerstone for spiritual growth, offering solace, guidance, and the strength to confront our inner demons. This relationship is not merely a religious construct; it is an essential lifeline that imbues our existence with purpose and direction. In the vast tapestries of Indian epic literature, particularly in *The Ramayana* and *The Mahabharata*, this divine connection plays a pivotal role, illustrating how divine intervention and wisdom empower individuals to navigate their inner turmoil and emerge victorious over their darker selves.

Divine Guidance in *The Ramayana*

In *The Ramayana*, the epic unfolds the life of Lord Rama, an incarnation of the divine, whose journey embodies righteousness, virtue, and the quest for truth. The narrative serves as a canvas for exploring the intricacies of the human condition, where divine guidance illuminates the path amidst chaos and despair.

When Rama is exiled to the forest, he faces profound challenges, not only in the form of external adversaries like Ravana but also within his own psyche. The relationship between Rama and his devoted companion Hanuman exemplifies the transformative power of divine connection. Hanuman, a celestial being with unwavering devotion, symbolizes the bridge between the divine and humanity. His unwavering faith propels Rama forward, reinforcing the belief that divine support can conquer the most formidable of inner demons—fear, doubt, and despair.

Consider the moment when Rama is on the brink of hopelessness after Sita's abduction. It is Hanuman's unwavering devotion and the divine blessings he carries that reignite Rama's courage. This reflects a profound truth: the connection to the divine, often facilitated through devotion and the grace of divine beings, becomes a source of strength that allows individuals to rise above their fears. The struggle against Ravana can be seen as a metaphor for conquering one's own ego and attachments, with Rama's journey illustrating how divine guidance can illuminate the path to inner liberation.

The Complexity of Dharma in *The Mahabharata*

Transitioning to *The Mahabharata*, we encounter a different yet equally compelling exploration of the divine-human connection. The epic intricately weaves the themes of dharma (righteousness) and adharma (unrighteousness), showcasing the tension between these forces within the human soul. At the heart of this narrative lies Lord Krishna, whose role as both charioteer and divine guide exemplifies the vital importance of connecting with the divine in moments of moral crisis.

The Bhagavad Gita, a profound dialogue between Arjuna and Krishna on the battlefield of Kurukshetra, encapsulates this connection beautifully. As Arjuna grapples with the moral dilemma of fighting against his own kin, he experiences a crisis that reflects the internal conflicts we all face. In this moment of despair, Krishna emerges as the voice of divine wisdom, urging Arjuna to confront his fears and duties with courage.

Krishna's teachings serve as a catalyst for Arjuna's transformation. The divine connection becomes a source of clarity amidst confusion, illustrating how surrendering to a higher power can illuminate the path to righteousness. Krishna does not merely offer solutions; he empowers Arjuna to recognize and confront his inner demons—the fear of loss, guilt, and the weight of responsibility. Through this engagement, the epic articulates a profound message: the divine does not remove our struggles but provides the wisdom and strength necessary to face them.

Conquering Inner Demons

Both epics illustrate that the divine is not a distant observer but an active participant in the struggles of life. The journey towards conquering inner demons often involves recognizing our limitations and seeking divine guidance to transcend them. In *The Ramayana*, the embodiment of virtue in Rama serves as a reminder that one can aspire to righteousness, even in the face of daunting challenges. In contrast, *The Mahabharata* presents the complexities of moral dilemmas, emphasizing the necessity of divine wisdom in navigating the intricacies of dharma.

The internal battles faced by Rama and Arjuna reflect universal themes of fear, doubt, and the search for meaning. The connection to the divine acts as a salve for these inner wounds, providing hope and strength. The characters in these epics demonstrate that the path to overcoming one's darker inclinations often requires humility—acknowledging that we are part of a larger cosmic order, where divine forces guide our actions and decisions.

The Role of Faith and Devotion

Faith and devotion emerge as vital elements in establishing a connection with the divine. In *The Ramayana*, the unwavering devotion of characters like Hanuman underscores how faith can elevate one's consciousness and foster resilience. Hanuman's leaps of faith, both literal and metaphorical, symbolize the journey of the soul toward divine union, where the individual transcends personal limitations through devotion.

Similarly, in *The Mahabharata*, Arjuna's eventual acceptance of Krishna as his divine guide encapsulates the importance of surrendering to a higher power. This act of surrender allows Arjuna to navigate his internal conflict with clarity and purpose. The Gita teaches that faith is not passive; it is an active engagement that transforms despair into strength, illuminating the way forward.

The Dance of Destiny and Free Will

Both epics also explore the delicate interplay between destiny and free will. The characters are often faced with circumstances seemingly dictated by fate; yet, their choices, guided by divine wisdom, shape their destinies. Rama's adherence to dharma, even when faced with exile and loss, reflects the profound understanding that personal choices, rooted in divine connection, can alter the course of one's life.

In *The Mahabharata*, Krishna's role as a divine strategist emphasizes the importance of making conscious choices even amidst predestined circumstances. Arjuna's eventual acceptance of his duty illustrates how, through the divine connection, individuals can align their actions with higher principles, allowing them to conquer not only their fears but also the forces of chaos that threaten their inner peace.

The Eternal Quest for Union with the Divine

Ultimately, the connection between humanity and the divine represents an eternal quest for union. Both *The Ramayana* and *The Mahabharata* convey that this connection is not merely about seeking assistance during times of struggle; it is about nurturing a relationship that fosters spiritual growth and inner transformation.

Rama's unwavering commitment to dharma and Arjuna's eventual embrace of his responsibilities reflect the dual aspects of this quest—living in accordance with divine principles while striving for self-realization. The divine becomes a mirror, reflecting the highest aspirations of the human spirit and guiding individuals toward their truest selves.

The Path to Inner Liberation

In the grand narratives of *The Ramayana* and *The Mahabharata*, the connection between humanity and the divine emerges as a vital theme, underscoring the importance of seeking divine guidance in our journey toward spiritual growth. As we grapple with our inner demons—fear, doubt, and moral dilemmas—the divine stands as a beacon of hope, illuminating the path toward inner liberation.

Through the stories of Rama and Arjuna, we learn that the divine does not absolve us of our struggles but empowers us to confront them with courage and clarity. This sacred connection, forged through faith and devotion, transforms our challenges into opportunities for growth, allowing us to transcend our limitations and realize our highest potential.

In the end, the dance between humanity and the divine is a testament to the resilience of the human spirit—a journey that calls us to seek, to question, and ultimately, to embrace the mystery of existence with grace and humility. As we cultivate this connection, we find not only the strength to conquer our inner demons but also the profound joy of becoming one with the divine essence that permeates all of creation.

Spirituality and Higher Consciousness: Pathways to Happiness

The quest for happiness is a universal pursuit, yet its definition varies across cultures and philosophies. In many spiritual traditions, including those found in the Puranas, the Vedas, *The Ramayana*, and *The Mahabharata*, happiness is linked to spirituality and the attainment of a higher level of consciousness. This connection fosters a deeper understanding of oneself, promotes inner peace, and cultivates a sense of unity with the cosmos. Here, we explore how spirituality facilitates this journey toward happiness, supported by insights from these ancient texts.

The Essence of Spirituality

Spirituality encompasses a broad range of practices and beliefs aimed at connecting with a higher power or truth. It often involves self-exploration, meditation, and ethical living, fostering an inner transformation that transcends material concerns. In the context of the Puranas and Vedic texts, spirituality is viewed as a pathway to understanding the nature of existence and one's place within it.

Vedic Insights on Higher Consciousness

The Vedas emphasize the importance of self-realization and the pursuit of knowledge (jnana) as essential to achieving happiness. The concept of *Brahman*, the ultimate reality, highlights that true happiness arises from recognizing our unity with this divine essence.

For instance, the *Chandogya Upanishad* teaches that understanding the self (*Atman*) as part of *Brahman* leads to liberation (*moksha*). This liberation is often equated with lasting happiness, as it frees individuals from the cycles of desire and suffering. By meditating on one's true nature and the interconnectedness of all beings, practitioners can cultivate a profound sense of peace and fulfillment that transcends the temporary joys of material existence.

The Role of Dharma in Happiness

The texts of *The Ramayana* and *The Mahabharata* elaborate on the significance of *dharma* (righteous duty) in achieving happiness. Both epics illustrate that living in accordance with one's moral and ethical obligations leads to harmony both within oneself and in society.

The Ramayana: Dharma and Devotion

In *The Ramayana*, the character of Rama exemplifies the principles of *dharma*. His commitment to righteousness, even in the face of adversity, underscores the belief that following one's duty fosters inner peace. When Rama is exiled, he faces challenges that test his resolve and character. However, his unwavering commitment to *dharma* not only strengthens his spirit but also inspires those around him.

Rama's relationship with Sita and his companions showcases how spiritual bonds can enhance happiness. Their loyalty and devotion provide emotional support, reminding us that connection and love are essential components of a fulfilling life. This narrative illustrates that when we align our actions with higher principles and nurture our relationships, we pave the way for deeper joy.

The Mahabharata: The Complexity of Choices

In *The Mahabharata*, the ethical dilemmas faced by characters such as Arjuna highlight the importance of making conscious choices that resonate with one's higher self. Arjuna's moment of crisis on the battlefield, where he hesitates to fight against his kin, serves as a metaphor for the inner conflicts we all experience.

Krishna's counsel emphasizes the need to rise above personal attachments and understand the larger cosmic order. By encouraging Arjuna to fulfill his duty as a warrior, Krishna illustrates that true happiness comes from selfless action and adhering to one's *dharma*. This lesson resonates with the idea that happiness is not merely a pursuit of personal pleasure but often involves sacrifice and a commitment to the greater good.

The Transformative Power of Meditation and Mindfulness

Both the Vedas and the Puranas advocate for practices like meditation and mindfulness as essential tools for achieving a higher state of consciousness. These practices cultivate awareness and presence, enabling individuals to connect with their inner selves and the universe.

Meditation in Vedic Traditions

The Vedic texts describe meditation as a means to quiet the mind, transcend the ego, and experience unity with the divine. The *Yoga Sutras of Patanjali* emphasize the importance of mental discipline in achieving *samadhi* (a state of deep meditative absorption). This state fosters profound inner peace, allowing individuals to experience joy that is not contingent on external circumstances.

For example, the practice of *dhyana* (meditative contemplation) leads to insights that help individuals understand the transient nature of worldly pleasures. This realization fosters a sense of detachment, allowing one to experience happiness that is independent of external factors. By cultivating inner stillness and clarity, meditation becomes a pathway to lasting fulfilment.

Mindfulness in Daily Life

The teachings found in the Puranas also emphasize the importance of mindfulness in everyday life. By being present and aware of our thoughts and actions, we cultivate a deeper understanding of our motivations and desires. This awareness can lead to more intentional living, reducing stress and enhancing overall well-being.

For instance, the practice of *puja* (worship) in the Puranas encourages individuals to engage mindfully in rituals that connect them to the divine. This act of devotion fosters a sense of purpose and belonging, contributing to emotional well-being and happiness.

The Joy of Service and Selflessness

Another significant theme across these texts is the value of selfless service (*seva*) as a pathway to happiness. Engaging in acts of kindness and compassion fosters a sense of fulfillment that transcends personal desires.

Examples from the Puranas

In the Puranas, numerous stories illustrate how selfless acts lead to spiritual elevation and happiness. For instance, the tale of King Harishchandra, who remained steadfast in his commitment to truth and righteousness, ultimately leads to his liberation from suffering. His willingness to sacrifice for the truth demonstrates that true happiness is found in living with integrity and serving others.

The Interconnectedness of All Beings

The teachings found in the Vedas, Puranas, and epics like *The Ramayana* and *The Mahabharata* highlight the interconnectedness of all beings, fostering compassion and empathy. Understanding this interconnectedness is crucial for attaining a higher level of consciousness.

Compassion in The Ramayana

In *The Ramayana*, the bond between Rama and his loyal devotee Hanuman exemplifies this interconnectedness. Hanuman's unwavering devotion and willingness to help others underscore the idea that happiness is amplified when we serve and uplift those around us. Their relationship illustrates that genuine love and support contribute to an individual's joy, creating a ripple effect of positivity in the world.

The Mahabharata's Teachings on Unity

Similarly, *The Mahabharata* conveys messages of unity and collective responsibility. The Kurukshetra War, though a conflict, ultimately leads to a deeper understanding of duty and the importance of standing together for righteousness. The lessons learned through this epic resonate in the notion that true happiness comes from fostering connections with others and recognizing our shared humanity.

The Journey Towards Self-Realization

Spirituality encourages self-exploration and self-realization, which are vital for achieving genuine happiness. The process of understanding oneself and aligning with one's true nature fosters a sense of peace and fulfillment.

Self-realisation in Vedic Philosophy

The Vedic texts advocate for introspection as a means to uncover one's true essence. The exploration of the self leads to the realization that happiness is not dependent on external circumstances but rather an intrinsic quality that can be accessed through spiritual practices.

In essence, self-realization involves understanding that we are more than our thoughts, emotions, and material possessions. By cultivating awareness of our true nature as interconnected beings, we can experience a profound sense of joy that is stable and enduring.

The Holistic Approach to Happiness

The teachings found in the Puranas, Vedas, *The Ramayana*, and *The Mahabharata* reveal that spirituality and the pursuit of a higher level of consciousness are essential for achieving happiness. By embracing the principles of *dharma*, engaging in meditation, practicing mindfulness, and fostering selflessness, individuals can cultivate inner peace and fulfillment.

Happiness, as depicted in these ancient texts, is not a fleeting emotion tied to external achievements but a deep-rooted state of being that arises from understanding our connection to the divine and to one another. This holistic approach encourages us to seek joy within, recognize our interdependence, and navigate life's complexities with grace and compassion.

In the end, the journey toward happiness is both an inward exploration and an outward expression of love and service. By embracing spirituality, we unlock the potential for profound joy that transcends the trials of existence, illuminating the path toward a more fulfilled and harmonious life

Part I:

Awakening the Inner Light: Cultivating Spiritual Energy and Power in Hindu Traditions

Developing Spiritual Energy and Power Within: Insights from Hindu Texts

Spiritual energy, often described as a vital force within, plays a crucial role in personal growth and enlightenment in Hindu philosophy. The ancient texts of Hinduism, including the Vedas, Upanishads, Puranas, *The Ramayana*, and *The Mahabharata*, provide a rich tapestry of teachings and practices designed to cultivate this inner power. This exploration seeks to outline the methodologies through which individuals can develop spiritual energy, drawing on these profound sources of wisdom.

Understanding Spiritual Energy

Spiritual energy can be understood as the life force or *prana* that animates all beings. In the Hindu context, it is the essence that connects the individual to the divine and the cosmos. This energy manifests in various forms, including creativity, intuition, and transformative power, allowing individuals to transcend the mundane and connect with higher states of consciousness.

The Concept of *Prana*

Prana, often translated as "life force," is central to understanding spiritual energy in Hinduism. It is considered the vital energy that sustains life, akin to the concept of *qi* in Chinese philosophy or *ki* in Japanese traditions. According to the *Yoga Sutras of Patanjali*, the mastery of *prana* is essential for spiritual development. Techniques to cultivate *prana* include breath control (*pranayama*), meditation, and ethical living (*yamas* and *niyamas*).

Pathways to Develop Spiritual Energy

The development of spiritual energy involves various practices and disciplines, which can be broadly categorized into three main areas: physical, mental, and spiritual. Each category encompasses specific techniques rooted in Hindu philosophy that can enhance one's spiritual power.

1. Physical Practices

Physical practices focus on the body as a vessel for spiritual energy. Maintaining physical health and vitality is crucial for spiritual development.

a. Yoga

Yoga is perhaps the most well-known physical practice associated with spiritual growth in Hinduism. Originating from ancient texts, yoga integrates body, mind, and spirit, facilitating the flow of *prana* within the body.

1. **Hatha Yoga**: This form of yoga emphasizes physical postures (*asanas*) and breath control (*pranayama*). Regular practice helps purify the body and mind, creating a conducive environment for spiritual growth. The *Hatha Yoga Pradipika*, an ancient text, outlines various *asanas* and their effects on the body and consciousness.
2. **Kundalini Yoga**: This practice focuses on awakening the dormant spiritual energy within, often visualized as a coiled serpent at the base of the spine. Techniques include specific postures, breath control, and meditation. The goal is to raise this energy through the chakras, leading to heightened states of awareness and spiritual power.

b. Pranayama (Breath Control)

Pranayama refers to the practice of controlling breath, which directly influences *prana* within the body. Various techniques can enhance spiritual energy:

1. **Nadi Shodhana** (Alternate Nostril Breathing): This technique balances the two hemispheres of the brain and purifies the energy channels (*nadis*), promoting mental clarity and tranquility.
2. **Kapalabhati** (Skull Shining Breath): A vigorous breathing technique that purifies the lungs and energizes the mind, preparing the practitioner for deeper meditation.

By mastering *pranayama*, individuals can significantly enhance their ability to harness and direct spiritual energy.

c. Diet and Lifestyle

Maintaining a pure and satvic diet (foods that promote harmony and health) is fundamental to developing spiritual energy. The *Bhagavad Gita* emphasizes the importance of wholesome food, suggesting that what we consume impacts our thoughts and spiritual progress. Foods such as fresh fruits, vegetables, whole grains, and nuts are considered beneficial for cultivating *sattva*, promoting clarity and peace.

2. Mental Practices

Mental practices are aimed at cultivating a focused, disciplined mind that is essential for spiritual growth.

a. Meditation

Meditation is a central practice in Hindu spirituality, providing the means to quiet the mind and connect with deeper layers of consciousness. Various forms of meditation include:

1. **Dhyana**: This form of meditation emphasizes single-pointed focus, often on a mantra or an image of the divine. Regular practice helps in calming the mind and accessing higher states of awareness.
2. **Bhakti Meditation**: Focusing on devotion to a personal deity, this form of meditation fosters a deep emotional connection to the divine, enhancing feelings of love, joy, and spiritual energy.
3. **Self-Inquiry**: Rooted in the teachings of the Upanishads, self-inquiry involves asking "Who am I?" to uncover the true nature of the self beyond the ego. This practice leads to profound realizations that energize the spirit.

b. Affirmations and Mantras

Using affirmations and mantras can amplify spiritual energy. Mantras, which are sacred sounds or phrases, have profound vibrational qualities that can transform consciousness. The *Gayatri Mantra* is a prime example, invoking divine illumination and fostering spiritual growth. Repeating mantras creates a vibrational resonance that enhances focus, intention, and spiritual energy.

c. Visualization

Visualization techniques involve imagining oneself in states of spiritual power, light, or unity with the divine. This practice, often used in conjunction with meditation, can energize the mind and facilitate a deeper connection with higher consciousness.

3. Spiritual Practices

Spiritual practices form the core of personal transformation and connection with the divine.

a. Dharma (Righteous Living)

Living according to *dharma*, or righteousness, is fundamental for cultivating spiritual energy. The *Bhagavad Gita* emphasizes that actions performed in alignment with *dharma* purify the soul and enhance spiritual power. By engaging in selfless actions and ethical living, individuals create a positive karmic foundation that supports spiritual development.

b. Seva (Selfless Service)

Engaging in *seva*, or selfless service, is a powerful way to cultivate spiritual energy. By serving others without attachment to outcomes, individuals transcend their ego and connect with the collective human experience. This practice fosters compassion and empathy, enriching one's spiritual journey. The stories from the Puranas often illustrate the transformative power of service, emphasizing that genuine happiness arises from giving and uplifting others.

c. Satsang (Company of the Wise)

Surrounding oneself with spiritually minded individuals is known as *satsang*. The energy generated in the presence of enlightened beings or sincere practitioners can uplift and inspire personal growth. Attending gatherings, discussions, and spiritual retreats creates an environment conducive to spiritual development.

The Role of Intention and Focus

Developing spiritual energy requires clarity of intention and focused effort. Setting a clear intention for spiritual growth establishes a roadmap for the journey ahead.

1. **Setting Intentions**: By articulating specific spiritual goals—such as achieving inner peace, deepening meditation practice, or developing compassion—individuals can align their actions with their aspirations. This clarity channels energy toward the desired outcome.
2. **Mindfulness and Presence**: Being present and mindful in everyday activities enhances awareness and helps individuals connect with their spiritual essence. The practice of mindfulness encourages individuals to

observe their thoughts and feelings without attachment, creating space for spiritual energy to flow.

The Significance of Guru and Spiritual Guidance

In Hindu tradition, the role of a *guru* (spiritual teacher) is paramount in developing spiritual energy. A *guru* provides guidance, wisdom, and support, helping disciples navigate the complexities of spiritual growth.

1. **Transmission of Energy**: The *guru* is believed to transmit spiritual energy to the disciple through teachings, blessings, and presence. This transmission can catalyze profound transformations, awakening latent spiritual power within.
2. **Personalized Guidance**: Each individual's spiritual journey is unique. A *guru* can provide tailored practices and advice based on the disciple's needs, ensuring that their path is aligned with their personal spiritual evolution.

The Power of Rituals and Sacred Practices

Rituals play an essential role in connecting individuals with spiritual energy. They create a sacred space and time, facilitating a deeper connection with the divine.

1. **Puja (Worship)**: Engaging in *puja* involves offering prayers, flowers, and food to deities, creating an atmosphere of devotion and reverence. This practice fosters a connection with the divine and allows spiritual energy to flow.
2. **Yajna (Sacrificial Fire)**: The practice of *yajna*, or fire sacrifice, is described in the Vedas as a means of invoking divine blessings. The sacred fire symbolizes transformation, and offerings made into the fire elevate one's spiritual energy and purify the environment.
3. **Festivals and Celebrations**: Participating in spiritual festivals and communal celebrations reinforces the connection to community and tradition. These occasions enhance collective energy, allowing individuals to partake in a shared spiritual experience.

The Journey of Inner Alchemy

Developing spiritual energy can be viewed as a process of inner alchemy—transforming the base aspects of the self into higher states of consciousness.

1. **Transmutation of Emotions**: Emotions like anger, fear, and desire can be transformed into spiritual energy through conscious awareness and practice. Techniques such as meditation and self-inquiry help individuals recognize and transmute these emotions into love and compassion.

2. **Balancing the Chakras**: The chakra system, described in various texts, offers a framework for understanding the flow of spiritual energy. Balancing the chakras through yoga, meditation, and energy work enhances the overall vitality of an individual, allowing for greater access to spiritual power.

Integrating Spiritual Practices into Daily Life

Integrating spiritual practices into daily life ensures that the development of spiritual energy becomes a continuous process.

1. **Daily Meditation**: Setting aside time each day for meditation cultivates consistency and allows individuals to deepen their practice, gradually enhancing their spiritual energy.
2. **Mindful Living**: Practicing mindfulness in daily activities—whether eating, working, or interacting with others—encourages a deeper connection to the present moment, fostering awareness and spiritual growth.
3. **Gratitude and Reflection**: Cultivating an attitude of gratitude allows individuals to appreciate life's blessings, promoting positive energy and reinforcing a spiritual outlook. Reflecting on personal experiences and lessons learned can provide insights for further growth.

Overcoming Obstacles to Spiritual Development

The path of spiritual development is not without challenges. Recognizing and addressing obstacles is essential for cultivating spiritual energy.

1. **Ego and Attachment**: The ego often acts as a barrier to spiritual growth. Practices like self-inquiry help individuals understand the nature of the ego and cultivate detachment from it, allowing for greater access to spiritual energy.
2. **Distractions and Mundanity**: The distractions of modern life can dilute spiritual practice. Creating a dedicated spiritual space, establishing routines, and prioritizing spiritual activities help mitigate these distractions.
3. **Self-Doubt**: Self-doubt can hinder progress on the spiritual path. Engaging in positive affirmations and seeking guidance from spiritual teachers can bolster confidence and reinforce one's commitment to growth.

The Path of Spiritual Empowerment

Developing spiritual energy and power within oneself is a transformative journey illuminated by the teachings of Hindu texts. Through a combination of physical practices, mental discipline, spiritual engagement, and community connection, individuals can awaken their inner potential.

This journey is not a destination but an ongoing process of discovery and growth. By integrating the principles of *dharma*, practicing meditation, engaging in selfless service, and cultivating mindfulness, individuals can access and amplify their spiritual energy. In doing so, they align themselves with the greater cosmic flow, experiencing a profound sense of joy, peace, and unity with all beings.

Ultimately, the development of spiritual energy empowers individuals to transcend their limitations, embrace their true essence, and contribute positively to the world. Through the guidance of ancient wisdom, one can embark on a path of spiritual awakening that fosters happiness, compassion, and a deeper connection to the divine.

The Importance of Brahmacharya: Sexual Energy Protection in Spiritual Ascension

Brahmacharya, often translated as celibacy or sexual restraint, is a vital principle in many spiritual traditions, including Hinduism. It encompasses not only abstinence from sexual activity but also the cultivation of discipline, control over desires, and a focus on higher spiritual goals. In the context of spiritual ascension, Brahmacharya is seen as a crucial element that enables individuals to conserve and transform their sexual energy into spiritual power. This essay explores the significance of Brahmacharya through the lives of key figures from the Hindu epics—Bhishma, Karna, Dronacharya, Arjuna, and Ravana—illuminating how their relationships with sexual energy shaped their destinies and spiritual paths.

Understanding Brahmacharya

Brahmacharya embodies the pursuit of spiritual knowledge and truth through the disciplined use of one's energy, particularly sexual energy.

In spiritual practice, sexual energy is viewed as a potent force that can either lead to distraction or be harnessed for enlightenment. Properly channelling this energy is essential for achieving higher states of consciousness. In the spiritual context, Brahmacharya involves:

1. **Control over Desires**: Mastery over one's impulses and desires, particularly sexual urges, which can distract from spiritual pursuits.
2. **Channeling Energy**: Transforming sexual energy into creative, intellectual, and spiritual endeavours.
3. **Fostering Inner Peace**: Cultivating a sense of tranquillity and clarity of mind that arises from discipline.

The Role of Brahmacharya in the Lives of Key Figures

Bhishma: The Ideal Celibate

Bhishma, one of the most revered characters in the *Mahabharata*, embodies the principle of Brahmacharya to its fullest. Born to Ganga and King Shantanu, Bhishma took a vow of celibacy to ensure his father's happiness and uphold his kingdom's stability. This vow not only shaped his life choices but also elevated his spiritual stature.

Spiritual Ascension Through Self-Denial: Bhishma's commitment to celibacy granted him extraordinary powers and wisdom. His control over sexual energy allowed him to cultivate profound insights into duty (*dharma*) and righteousness. The energy that would have been spent on personal desires was redirected into his roles as a warrior and a protector of his family and kingdom.

Consequences of Sexual Energy: Despite his exemplary adherence to Brahmacharya, Bhishma's life is also marked by the consequences of desire. His love for his mother Ganga and his loyalty to the throne led to a complex relationship with duty and sacrifice. His ultimate downfall during the Kurukshetra War serves as a reminder that even those who practice Brahmacharya must remain vigilant about the subtler forms of attachment.

Karna: The Tragic Hero

Karna, another significant character in the *Mahabharata*, presents a contrasting example. Known for his unwavering loyalty and martial prowess, Karna struggled with his desires and the societal stigma surrounding his birth. His relationship with sexual energy is multifaceted, characterized by both mastery and eventual tragedy.

Harnessing Energy for Valor: While Karna did not strictly adhere to Brahmacharya, his dedication to his principles and friendships gave him immense strength. His love for Draupadi, even if unfulfilled, reflected a yearning that could have diverted him from his path. The energy he expended in pursuing honor and recognition as a warrior, however, manifested as courage and resilience on the battlefield.

The Downfall of Desire: Karna's attachment to his status and his rivalry with Arjuna ultimately led to his downfall. The choices he made—guided by his desires rather than spiritual discipline—culminated in a tragic fate. His failure to embrace Brahmacharya fully highlights the risks associated with unchecked desires, serving as a cautionary tale about the consequences of mismanaged sexual energy.

Dronacharya: The Teacher's Dilemma

Dronacharya, the revered teacher of the Kauravas and Pandavas, presents another perspective on Brahmacharya. As a Brahmin and a teacher, Dronacharya's role was pivotal in shaping the next generation of warriors. His adherence to discipline and control over desires was critical in his journey, but he faced unique challenges.

Discipline in Teaching: Dronacharya exemplified the principles of Brahmacharya through his commitment to his students. His teachings were imbued with a sense of duty, and he instilled in his disciples the importance of discipline and focus. His sexual energy was channeled into his role as a teacher, creating a profound impact on the warriors he trained.

Attachment and Consequences: However, Dronacharya's attachment to his students, particularly his affection for Ashwatthama, and his desire for recognition clouded his judgment during the war. When faced with the loss of his son, his emotional turmoil led to a lapse in his discipline, which ultimately contributed to his tragic fate. This serves as a reminder that even those who espouse Brahmacharya can fall prey to attachment and desire if not vigilant.

Arjuna: The Struggles of the Ideal Warrior

Arjuna, the central character of the *Mahabharata*, embodies the dual nature of Brahmacharya: the struggle between physical desires and spiritual duties. His journey illustrates the challenges of mastering sexual energy in the pursuit of higher ideals.

Focus and Dedication: Arjuna's commitment to his training and mastery of archery exemplifies a form of Brahmacharya. His single-minded focus on becoming a great warrior allowed him to develop incredible skill and power. In his moments of meditation and practice, he redirected his sexual energy toward his martial goals.

Temptations and Lessons: However, Arjuna faced significant temptations, particularly in his relationships with women. His love for Draupadi and the allure of romantic pursuits posed challenges to his discipline. The turning point in his life came during the Kurukshetra War, where Krishna's guidance helped him realign his focus with his higher purpose. Krishna's teachings emphasize that Brahmacharya is not solely about physical restraint but also about channelling one's energies toward dharma and self-realization.

Ravana: The Perils of Unrestrained Desire

Ravana, the demon king of Lanka, serves as a contrasting figure to the ideals of Brahmacharya. His story illustrates the destructive consequences of unchecked sexual energy and desire.

Power and Lust: Despite his formidable strengths and knowledge, Ravana's downfall was rooted in his inability to control his desires. His lust for Sita led him to abduct her, igniting a war with Rama. Ravana's actions reflect a failure to practice Brahmacharya, as his desires led to moral corruption and chaos.

Consequences of Ignorance: The tale of Ravana highlights the spiritual consequences of unrestrained sexual energy. While he possessed immense power and wisdom, his inability to channel this energy for constructive purposes resulted in his ultimate destruction. His story serves as a cautionary tale about the importance of Brahmacharya in maintaining spiritual integrity and power.

The Spiritual Dimension of Brahmacharya

The practice of Brahmacharya goes beyond mere abstinence; it is a pathway to spiritual awakening. By cultivating control over sexual energy, individuals can experience profound transformations:

1. **Enhanced Concentration**: Sexual energy, when conserved, can enhance mental clarity and focus, allowing for deeper meditation and spiritual practices.
2. **Increased Vitality**: Restraining sexual impulses can lead to increased physical and mental vitality, facilitating greater engagement in spiritual activities.
3. **Inner Peace**: Mastery over desires promotes a sense of inner tranquility, freeing individuals from the turmoil that often accompanies unfulfilled cravings.

Practical Steps to Cultivate Brahmacharya

1. **Mindfulness and Awareness**: Practicing mindfulness can help individuals become aware of their desires and impulses. This awareness is the first step toward mastery and control.
2. **Mantra Sadhana and Breath Control**: Regular Mantra Sadhana and pranayama can help channel sexual energy into spiritual practices, fostering a deeper connection with oneself and the divine.
3. **Ethical Living**: Living in accordance with *dharma* reinforces the principles of Brahmacharya, aligning one's actions with spiritual goals.
4. **Community and Support**: Engaging with like-minded individuals who value spiritual growth can provide encouragement and accountability in the practice of Brahmacharya.

The Path of Spiritual Ascension

Brahmacharya is a powerful principle that can lead to spiritual ascension when practiced with sincerity and dedication. Through the examples of Bhishma, Karna, Dronacharya, Arjuna, and Ravana, we see the varied implications of sexual energy in shaping destinies.

Ultimately, the path of Brahmacharya is one of self-discovery, discipline, and transformation. By mastering sexual energy, individuals can transcend their limitations, realize their true potential, and align with their higher selves. This practice not only enriches one's spiritual journey but also contributes to a more harmonious existence, fostering peace, joy, and connection with the universe.

Part II:

Mantra Sadhana: The Art of Spiritual Practice

Mantra Sadhana is a profound spiritual practice rooted in the ancient traditions of Hinduism, particularly as described in the Vedas and Puranas. It involves the repetition of specific sounds or phrases—mantras—with the intention of invoking divine energies, focusing the mind, and facilitating spiritual growth. This exploration delves into the essence of Mantra Sadhana, its significance, methodologies, and the wisdom shared by revered figures like Rajashri Nandi and Bhavesh Yuj.

Understanding Mantras

The Nature of Mantras

Mantras are sacred syllables, words, or phrases believed to embody divine energies. Derived from the Sanskrit root "man," which means "to think," and "tra," meaning "to protect," a mantra serves as a tool for mental protection and spiritual elevation.

Mantras are categorized into different types:

1. **Beej Mantras**: These are seed sounds that encapsulate the essence of deities and cosmic energies. For example, the beej mantra "Aim" represents Saraswati, the goddess of knowledge.
2. **Sankalpa Mantras**: These are intention-setting mantras used to align one's desires with spiritual goals.
3. **Shloka Mantras**: Longer verses, often drawn from scriptures, that convey profound teachings or invoke specific divine qualities.

The Importance of Sound Vibration

The significance of sound in Mantra Sadhana cannot be overstated. Each mantra's vibration resonates with particular frequencies that can influence the practitioner's mind and environment. The *Vedas* assert that sound is a fundamental aspect of creation. In the *Rigveda*, it is said:

"In the beginning was the Word (Nada), and the Word was with God."

This underscores the belief that sound has the power to shape reality.

Mantra Sadhana: The Practice

The Purpose of Mantra Sadhana

Mantra Sadhana serves multiple purposes:

1. **Mental Focus**: Repeating mantras helps concentrate the mind, diminishing distractions and fostering a state of mindfulness.
2. **Spiritual Connection**: Mantras are a means of connecting with divine energies, allowing practitioners to invoke blessings and guidance.
3. **Transformative Power**: Regular practice can lead to personal transformation, purifying the mind and spirit.

Steps in Mantra Sadhana

1. Preparation

Preparation is crucial for effective Mantra Sadhana. This includes creating a conducive environment, adopting a clean and comfortable posture, and entering a focused state of mind.

- **Setting the Space**: The practitioner should choose a quiet place, ideally adorned with sacred symbols, images of deities, and incense. This creates an atmosphere that encourages devotion and focus.
- **Adopting a Posture**: A comfortable seated position, such as Padmasana (Lotus Pose) or Sukhasana (Easy Pose), is recommended to facilitate relaxation and concentration.

2. Invocation

The practice begins with an invocation to the divine or the teacher (Guru). This can include reciting a specific shloka or offering prayers to set the intention for the practice.

3. Chanting the Mantra

Chanting the mantra can be done in various ways:

- **Loudly**: Vocalizing the mantra with clarity allows the vibrations to resonate outward, impacting the surrounding space.
- **Softly**: Whispering the mantra cultivates intimacy and focus within oneself.
- **Internally**: Silent repetition focuses the mind entirely on the mantra, allowing for deep introspection.

The repetition of the mantra can follow a specific count, often using a mala (prayer beads) to keep track.

4. Meditation

After chanting, practitioners often engage in meditation, allowing the vibrations of the mantra to permeate their consciousness. This is a time for reflection, connection, and surrender.

The Role of Breath

Breath control (Pranayama) plays a significant role in Mantra Sadhana. Coordinating breath with the chanting of mantras enhances the effectiveness of the practice. For example, inhaling deeply before chanting and exhaling during the chant can amplify the energy flow.

Wisdom from Rajashri Nandi and Bhavesh Yuj

Rajashri Nandi, a renowned figure in spiritual literature, emphasizes the transformative power of mantras. He stated:

"The sound of a mantra is not merely a vibration; it is a bridge between the earthly and the divine."

This highlights the notion that mantras serve as conduits for spiritual energy, allowing practitioners to transcend ordinary experiences.

Bhavesh Yuj, another influential spiritual teacher, speaks about the significance of intention in Mantra Sadhana. He remarked:

"It is not the quantity of repetitions but the quality of intention behind each utterance that determines the efficacy of the mantra."

This underscores the importance of sincerity and focus, suggesting that heartfelt practice can yield profound results, regardless of the number of repetitions.

Mantras in the Vedas and Puranas

Vedic Perspectives

The *Vedas*—the oldest sacred texts of Hinduism—extensively discuss the power of sound and mantra. The *Rigveda*, in particular, contains numerous hymns dedicated to various deities, illustrating the relationship between sound, intention, and divine presence.

- **Hymns of Invocation**: Vedic mantras often begin with invocations to deities like Agni (the fire god) or Indra (the king of gods), emphasizing the need for divine assistance and guidance.
- **Sama Veda**: This Veda is primarily concerned with melodies and chants, reinforcing the idea that musicality in mantra recitation enhances its spiritual potency.

Insights from the Puranas

The Puranas offer rich narratives and teachings on the practical application of mantras.

1. **The Devi Bhagavata Purana**: This text discusses the power of the *Durga Saptashati*, a collection of mantras that invoke the Goddess Durga. Practitioners believe that reciting these verses with devotion can lead to liberation

from obstacles and empower the individual with strength.
2. **The Vishnu Purana**: It emphasizes the recitation of the *Gayatri Mantra*, considered one of the most powerful mantras in Hinduism. This mantra is dedicated to the sun deity and is believed to provide wisdom, enlightenment, and protection.
3. **The Shiva Purana**: It highlights the significance of chanting *Om Namah Shivaya*, a mantra dedicated to Lord Shiva. This mantra embodies the essence of Shiva and is believed to bring inner peace and spiritual awakening.

The Transformational Power of Mantra

Mantra Sadhana not only serves individual practitioners but also contributes to collective spiritual energy. When individuals come together to chant mantras, the cumulative vibrations create a powerful environment conducive to transformation and healing.

Collective Chanting

In many spiritual traditions, collective chanting, or *sankirtan*, amplifies the effects of Mantra Sadhana. The energy generated during group practice fosters a sense of unity and community while deepening individual experiences.

Challenges in Practice

While Mantra Sadhana is profoundly rewarding, practitioners often face challenges, including:

1. **Distractions**: The wandering mind can hinder concentration. Techniques such as focusing on breath or visualization can help maintain focus.
2. **Impatience**: Results from Mantra Sadhana may not be immediate. Patience and consistency are essential for deeper experiences.
3. **Misunderstanding**: Some may approach mantra chanting as a mere ritual without understanding its spiritual significance. Education and guidance can help deepen the practice.

The Fruits of Mantra Sadhana

The benefits of regular Mantra Sadhana are manifold:

1. **Inner Peace**: The practice cultivates a sense of calm and tranquility, reducing stress and anxiety.
2. **Clarity of Mind**: Enhanced focus and mental clarity emerge from consistent practice, aiding decision-making and creativity.
3. **Spiritual Growth**: The transformation of energy fosters a deeper connection to the self and the divine, facilitating spiritual evolution.

Mantra Sadhana is a powerful spiritual practice that transcends mere repetition of sounds. Rooted in the wisdom of the Vedas and Puranas, it provides practitioners with tools to connect with divine energies, cultivate inner peace, and embark on a journey of self-discovery.

As Rajashri Nandi aptly stated, "The sound of a mantra is a bridge between the earthly and the divine." Through sincere and dedicated practice, individuals can harness the transformative power of mantras, channelling their energies toward spiritual ascension and the realization of their true selves.

In a world filled with distractions and challenges, Mantra Sadhana offers a timeless path to inner fulfilment, peace, and enlightenment. By embracing this sacred practice, individuals can navigate their spiritual journeys with grace, wisdom, and a deep connection to the divine.

Part III:

Detachment as a means to be more Spiritual

The Alchemy of Detachment: A Journey Toward Spiritual Growth and True Happiness

In the labyrinth of human experience, detachment emerges as a profound key—a transformative force that propels us toward deeper spiritual growth and genuine happiness. Often misunderstood as apathy, this enigmatic quality is a sacred art of balancing engagement with the world while remaining anchored in an inner sanctuary of peace. To embrace detachment is to embark on a journey of self-discovery, illuminating the path to a richer, more meaningful existence.

The Essence of Detachment

At its core, detachment allows us to step back from the incessant clamour of desires, expectations, and attachments that often cloud our vision. In a society that celebrates materialism and the relentless pursuit of success, detachment invites us to question the very foundations of our happiness. What are we truly seeking? Is it the fleeting satisfaction of material gains or the deeper fulfilment that arises from inner tranquillity? By disentangling ourselves from external influences, we cultivate a clarity that reveals our true essence.

Spiritual Growth Through Self-Discovery

When we practice detachment, we create space for introspection and self-awareness. This is where spiritual growth begins. In the stillness that accompanies detachment, we confront the layers of our identity—those masks we wear to navigate the world. Often, we find ourselves entangled in roles defined by societal expectations and personal ambitions. However, when we allow ourselves the grace of detachment, we can peel back these layers, confronting our innermost selves. This process, though unsettling, illuminates our true nature.

The Bhagavad Gita eloquently encapsulates this journey. In its verses, Krishna advises Arjuna to perform his duty without attachment to the results. This teaching of "Nishkama Karma" (selfless action) highlights how true spiritual growth arises when we act according to our dharma, free from the desire for outcomes. This principle encourages us to engage fully in our lives while cultivating detachment from the fruits of our actions, fostering a deeper sense of purpose.

The Balance of Engagement and Detachment

Detachment is not synonymous with indifference; rather, it embodies deep engagement with life that is free from the fetters of attachment. By cultivating this quality, we begin to perceive the world through a lens of compassion and understanding. We learn to appreciate the transient beauty of relationships and experiences without clinging to them for validation.

In the Mahabharata, the character of Yudhishthira exemplifies this balance. Despite the great turmoil surrounding the war, he embodies righteousness while remaining detached from the outcome, understanding that his duty is to uphold dharma. His resilience illustrates that true strength lies not in attachment to victory but in the commitment to what is just and right.

Resilience Through Detachment

As we deepen our practice of detachment, we find that it serves as a catalyst for resilience. Life's inevitable ups and downs can feel overwhelming. However, cultivating a detached outlook enables us to navigate challenges with grace. Instead of being swept away by emotional tides, we can observe our feelings, recognizing them as temporary waves rather than permanent fixtures.

The story of Prahlada in the Bhagavata Purana illustrates this resilience. Despite facing immense persecution from his father, Hiranyakashipu, for his devotion to Lord Vishnu, Prahlada remains steadfast.

His unwavering faith, grounded in detachment from fear and attachment to worldly power, serves as a testament to inner strength in the face of adversity.

Redefining Desire

Detachment allows us to redefine our relationship with desire. In a culture that equates happiness with the fulfillment of wants, we begin to explore the motivations behind our cravings—be they for possessions, recognition, or love. By examining these desires, we discern which arise from our authentic selves and which are echoes of societal conditioning.

The Yoga Sutras of Patanjali emphasize this exploration through the concept of "Santosha," or contentment. By cultivating contentment with what we have, we detach from the constant chase of desires, allowing us to experience a more profound sense of joy that is not contingent on external circumstances.

The True Source of Happiness

In this exploration of desire, we uncover the deeper source of true happiness. Freeing ourselves from attachments shifts our focus from external validation to inner contentment. This transition is not merely psychological; it represents a profound spiritual awakening. Happiness is not found in the accumulation of things or approval from others, but in the acceptance of ourselves and our place in the universe.

The teachings of the Upanishads resonate deeply with this realization. They urge us to recognize the oneness of the Atman (the self) with Brahman (the universal consciousness). This understanding fosters a profound sense of inner peace, as we come to realize that our true essence transcends worldly attachments and desires.

The Role of Detachment in Relationships

Detachment also transforms our relationships, enabling us to engage with others authentically. By freeing ourselves from the need to possess or control, we can experience love without fear. This dynamic fosters healthier connections, allowing relationships to flourish without the burden of expectations.

In the Ramayana, the relationship between Rama and Sita exemplifies this balance. Rama's unwavering commitment to dharma, even in the face of personal loss, illustrates how love can exist alongside detachment. His actions are guided by duty and righteousness rather than possessiveness, leading to a deep and abiding connection with Sita.

Embracing the Transience of Life

Ultimately, detachment teaches us to embrace the transient nature of life. Everything we experience is impermanent, from our relationships to our emotions. When we accept this reality, we cultivate a profound sense of freedom. Instead of clinging to moments, we learn to savor them, understanding that their beauty lies in their fleeting nature.

The teachings of Buddha resonate with this understanding. The concept of "Anicca," or impermanence, underscores the importance of recognizing the transient nature of all phenomena. By embracing impermanence, we cultivate a sense of liberation, allowing us to engage with life fully while remaining detached from its outcomes.

The Path to Spiritual Fulfillment

As we navigate our spiritual journeys, detachment becomes an essential compass. It guides us toward self-awareness, resilience, and true happiness. By cultivating this quality, we learn to dance gracefully with life's rhythms, engaging deeply while remaining rooted in our inner sanctum of peace.

In the end, the alchemy of detachment transforms our experience of existence. It liberates us from the shackles of attachment, enabling us to embrace the fullness of life with an open heart. As we embark on this journey, we discover that true happiness lies not in the accumulation of external treasures but in the richness of our inner world—a realm where peace, joy, and love reside in abundance. Through detachment, we unveil the profound beauty of our spiritual essence, guiding us toward a life of authentic fulfilment.

The Alchemy of Detachment: A Journey Toward Spiritual Growth and True Happiness

In the labyrinth of human experience, detachment emerges as a profound key—a transformative force that has the potential to propel us toward deeper spiritual growth and genuine happiness. This enigmatic quality, often misunderstood as apathy or disconnection, is, in fact, a sacred art of balancing engagement with the world while remaining anchored in an inner sanctuary of peace. To embrace detachment is to embark on a journey of self-discovery, illuminating the path to a richer, more meaningful existence.

At its core, detachment allows us to step back from the incessant clamor of desires, expectations, and attachments that often cloud our vision. In a society that celebrates materialism and the relentless pursuit of success, the notion of detachment invites us to question the very foundations of our happiness. What are we truly seeking? Is it the fleeting satisfaction of material gains or the deeper fulfillment that arises from inner tranquility? By disentangling ourselves from the myriad of external influences, we can cultivate a sense of clarity that reveals our true essence.

When we practice detachment, we create space for introspection and self-awareness. This is where spiritual growth begins. In the stillness that accompanies detachment, we can confront the layers of our identity—those masks we wear to navigate the world. We often find ourselves entangled in roles defined by societal expectations, familial obligations, and personal ambitions. Yet, when we allow ourselves the grace of detachment, we can peel back these layers and confront our innermost selves. This process can be unsettling, as we may discover aspects of ourselves that we have long ignored or suppressed. However, it is through this confrontation that we gain clarity, allowing the light of our true nature to emerge.

Detachment is not synonymous with indifference; rather, it embodies a deep engagement with life that is free from the fetters of attachment. When we cultivate this quality, we begin to perceive the world through a lens of compassion and understanding. We learn to appreciate the transient beauty of relationships and experiences without clinging to them for validation or security. This shift in perspective fosters a sense of interconnectedness, allowing us to see ourselves in others and others in ourselves. In this way, detachment becomes a bridge that unites us with the greater tapestry of existence, promoting empathy and kindness.

As we deepen our practice of detachment, we find that it serves as a catalyst for resilience. Life, with its inevitable ups and downs, can often feel overwhelming. However, when we cultivate a detached outlook, we gain the ability to navigate challenges with grace. Instead of being swept away by the tide of our emotions, we can observe our feelings from a distance, understanding that they are temporary waves rather than permanent fixtures. This perspective fosters emotional stability and empowers us to respond to life's trials with equanimity, rather than reactive despair or frustration.

Moreover, detachment allows us to redefine our relationship with desire. In a culture that often equates happiness with the fulfillment of wants, detachment invites us to explore the nature of our desires themselves. By stepping back and examining the motivations behind our cravings—be they for possessions, recognition, or love—we can discern which desires stem from our authentic selves and which are merely echoes of societal conditioning. This discernment is essential for spiritual growth, as it enables us to align our actions with our true values, fostering a sense of integrity and authenticity.

In this exploration of desire, we begin to uncover the deeper source of true happiness. When we free ourselves from the clutches of attachment, we shift our focus from external validation to inner contentment. This transition is not merely a psychological shift; it is a profound spiritual awakening. We begin to recognize that happiness is not found in the accumulation of things or the

The Detachment of Lord Rama: A Journey Toward Spiritual Growth and True Happiness

In the vast tapestry of Hindu mythology, few figures resonate as deeply as Lord Rama. His life, vividly chronicled in the epic Ramayana, embodies the principles of dharma (righteousness) and detachment, offering profound lessons for spiritual growth and genuine happiness. Rama's journey invites us into a world where duty intertwines with sacrifice, love is interlaced with respect, and detachment becomes a pathway to deeper understanding.

The Essence of Detachment

Detachment, in the spiritual context, is a nuanced quality. It does not imply indifference or disengagement; rather, it reflects a profound engagement with life that prioritizes duty over personal desires. This duality is beautifully encapsulated in Lord Rama's life—a life marked by devotion, honor, and unwavering commitment to righteousness.

As we delve into Rama's story, we encounter the concept of detachment as an art form, a skill that allows one to navigate the complexities of existence while remaining anchored in the essence of one's true self. It invites us to explore the delicate balance between involvement and emotional freedom, revealing the transformative power that lies within this equilibrium.

The Royal Birth and Early Life

Rama was born in Ayodhya to King Dasharatha and Queen Kausalya, a child destined for greatness. His arrival was not merely a familial joy but a fulfillment of divine prophecy—a promise to restore dharma in the world. From the moment of his birth, Rama's life was steeped in expectations and responsibilities. He was not just a prince; he was the embodiment of righteousness.

In his early years, Rama exhibited qualities that foreshadowed his future as an ideal king. His education in the sacred texts, archery, and martial arts prepared him for the trials that lay ahead. Yet, even in these formative years, he displayed a remarkable capacity for detachment. While he excelled in every endeavour, his focus was never on personal glory but on serving his family and community.

This early demonstration of detachment set the stage for his later actions. It is within this framework that we begin to understand the essence of Rama's character—a being deeply connected to his purpose, yet free from the shackles of ego and ambition.

The Call of Duty: Exile and Sacrifice

The turning point in Rama's life occurs when he is poised to ascend the throne of Ayodhya. However, fate intervenes in the form of his stepmother, Kaikeyi, who demands that her own son, Bharata, be crowned king instead. In a moment that tests the very fabric of his being, Rama chooses to accept exile over challenging his father's promise to Kaikeyi.

This decision reflects profound detachment. Rama prioritizes his father's honour over his own desires and rightful claim to the throne. It is a testament to his understanding that true kingship lies not in titles or power but in the fulfilment of one's dharma. His acceptance of exile is not an act of submission; it is a powerful assertion of integrity, demonstrating that he is guided by a higher purpose.

In the forests of exile, Rama, accompanied by Sita and his loyal brother Lakshmana, faces trials that further deepen his understanding of detachment. The wilderness, both beautiful and treacherous, becomes a crucible for his spiritual growth. Here, Rama learns to embrace simplicity and find joy in the moment, free from the trappings of royal life.

Trials in the Forest

The forest, with its myriad challenges, serves as a backdrop for Rama's evolution. He encounters sages, demons, and various beings, each interaction reinforcing his commitment to dharma. These experiences reveal the interconnectedness of life and the importance of compassion, further enriching his spiritual journey.

Rama's encounters with sages like Vishwamitra highlight the significance of mentorship and guidance on the path to enlightenment. Through these interactions, he learns to navigate the complexities of human emotion while maintaining an unwavering commitment to his principles. The teachings imparted by the sages serve as guiding stars, illuminating the way forward.

During these trials, the bond between Rama and Sita deepens. Their relationship, rooted in mutual respect and understanding, exemplifies the idea that love can flourish alongside detachment. Rama's unwavering devotion to Sita reflects his acknowledgment of her autonomy and dignity. He loves her not as a possession but as an equal partner in their shared journey.

The Abduction of Sita

The narrative takes a dramatic turn with the abduction of Sita by Ravana, the demon king of Lanka. This event serves as a pivotal moment, testing Rama's resolve and commitment to dharma. His response to this profound loss exemplifies the essence of emotional detachment—while he grieves for Sita, he channels his sorrow into action.

Rama's quest to rescue Sita is not driven by possessiveness but by a sense of duty to protect her honor. He enlists the help of allies, including Hanuman and the vanaras (monkey warriors), illustrating the importance of collaboration and community in overcoming adversity. This alliance reflects a broader understanding of detachment; while Rama is committed to his mission, he recognizes the value of support and connection.

The battle against Ravana is not merely a conflict; it is a symbolic representation of the struggle between dharma and adharma (unrighteousness). Rama's detachment allows him to approach this conflict with clarity and purpose, embodying the qualities of a true hero. He fights not for personal vengeance but for the restoration of balance and righteousness in the world.

The Return to Ayodhya

The climactic battle culminates in the defeat of Ravana, and Rama is finally reunited with Sita. However, their return to Ayodhya is not without its challenges. Despite his victory, Rama faces skepticism and doubt regarding Sita's chastity during her captivity. This moment reflects the complexities of societal expectations and the burdens of leadership.

In response to the whispers of the people, Rama demonstrates profound detachment. He places his duty to the kingdom above his personal desires and, with a heavy heart, asks Sita to undergo a trial by fire (Agni Pariksha) to prove her purity. This decision, though heart-wrenching, underscores the weight of dharma that rests upon a ruler's shoulders.

Sita's trial is a moment of intense emotional turmoil. Yet, her unwavering strength and resilience shine through, as she emerges unscathed, symbolizing the triumph of virtue over adversity. This episode highlights the intricate interplay between duty, honor, and the trials of leadership—elements that are inextricably linked to the concept of detachment.

The Reign of Rama: Ideal Kingship

Upon returning to Ayodhya, Rama is crowned king, fulfilling his destiny. His reign is marked by justice, prosperity, and peace, establishing him as the ideal ruler. However, his detachment remains central to his governance. He leads with compassion, ensuring the well-being of his subjects while remaining grounded in the principles of dharma.

The ideals of Rama Rajya (the reign of Rama) epitomize the harmony and righteousness that arise from a leader's commitment to detachment. His focus is not on personal glory or power but on serving his people with integrity and grace. This approach fosters a sense of unity and trust, allowing the kingdom to flourish.

Detachment in Relationships

Rama's relationships exemplify the essence of love intertwined with detachment. His bond with Sita, though deep and profound, is marked by mutual respect for each other's autonomy. They embody a partnership that transcends possessiveness, illustrating that true love is rooted in freedom and understanding.

Rama's relationship with Lakshmana, his loyal brother, further emphasizes this theme. Their companionship is characterized by unwavering loyalty and support, yet it is free from the need for control or domination. This dynamic reflects the idea that detachment does not equate to emotional distance; rather, it fosters healthy relationships grounded in trust and mutual growth.

The character of Hanuman also embodies this principle. As Rama's devoted disciple, Hanuman serves as a powerful example of love expressed through selfless service. His unwavering commitment to Rama showcases how detachment can manifest in profound loyalty, illustrating the beauty of relationships that thrive on mutual respect and shared purpose.

Embracing Impermanence

Throughout his journey, Rama encounters the impermanence of life—a theme that resonates deeply in the spiritual realm. The fleeting nature of joy and sorrow, love and loss, becomes a central aspect of his understanding. By embracing this impermanence, Rama cultivates a profound sense of acceptance, allowing him to navigate the complexities of existence with grace.

The final chapters of the Ramayana reveal the transient nature of even the most cherished relationships. Despite the joy of reunion, Rama must ultimately confront the inevitability of separation. Sita's eventual departure to the Earth reflects the ultimate truth of existence—that all things are subject to change. Rama's response to this loss is steeped in detachment, allowing him to honor Sita's journey while accepting the natural flow of life.

The Legacy of Lord Rama

The life of Lord Rama stands as a testament to the transformative power of detachment. His journey illustrates that spiritual growth is not merely about personal enlightenment but also about fulfilling one's responsibilities with grace and integrity. Rama's unwavering commitment to dharma serves as a guiding light for those seeking to navigate the complexities of life.

Through his experiences, we learn that detachment enables us to engage fully in our lives while remaining anchored in our true selves. It invites us to redefine our relationships, cultivate resilience, and embrace the impermanence of existence. In doing so, we discover the deeper source of true happiness—an inner contentment that transcends external circumstances.

Rama's legacy inspires us to reflect on our own lives, encouraging us to embody the qualities of love, duty, and detachment. His story serves as a timeless reminder that true fulfillment lies in the alignment of our actions with higher principles, guiding us toward a life of authenticity and purpose.

The Path Forward

In conclusion, the narrative of Lord Rama encapsulates the profound wisdom that emerges from the practice of detachment. His journey teaches us that spiritual growth and genuine happiness are intertwined with our ability to navigate the complexities of existence while remaining true to our higher selves.

As we reflect on Rama's life, we are invited to embrace our own journeys with an open heart. By cultivating detachment, we can engage deeply with our responsibilities, nurture authentic relationships, and find joy in the transient beauty of life. In doing so, we uncover the essence of our being—a place where peace, love, and fulfilment reside, guiding us toward a life of profound meaning and purpose.

Rama's story, steeped in elegance and mystery, continues to resonate, inviting each of us to embark on our own path toward spiritual enlightenment and true happiness. In the dance of existence, let us strive to embody the qualities that Lord Rama exemplified—commitment to dharma, resilience in adversity, and the grace of loving detachment. Through this journey, we may find the deeper truths that lie within us, illuminating our way toward a life of authentic fulfilment.

The Fulfillment of Selfless Devotion to God in Hindu Philosophy

In the vast and intricate tapestry of Hindu philosophy, the concept of selfless devotion to God, known as **bhakti**, stands as a transformative force that guides individuals toward profound fulfillment. This devotion is not merely an emotional expression but a holistic practice that intertwines spirituality with the pursuit of morality, wealth, and overall well-being. Through the exploration of various Hindu texts, we can delve into how selfless devotion enriches lives and fosters a sense of completeness.

Understanding Bhakti: The Path of Devotion

Bhakti originates from the Sanskrit root "bhaj," meaning "to adore" or "to worship." It emphasizes a personal, heartfelt connection with the divine. Unlike other spiritual paths that may focus on knowledge (jnana) or rigorous practices (karma), bhakti highlights an emotional engagement with God. This relationship transcends ritualistic worship and invites devotees into a profound communion with the divine.

The **Bhagavad Gita**, **Bhagavata Purana**, and the **Ramayana** are foundational texts that elucidate the significance of bhakti. Each of these scriptures provides insight into how selfless devotion leads to spiritual awakening and fulfillment in various aspects of life.

Morality: The Foundation of a Righteous Life

One of the foremost benefits of selfless devotion is the cultivation of morality. The relationship between a devotee and God is built on trust, love, and ethical conduct, leading to a life that reflects moral values.

1. **Alignment with Dharma**: The concept of **dharma** is central to Hindu philosophy, representing the moral and ethical duties that govern individual conduct. In the **Bhagavad Gita**, Lord Krishna emphasizes the importance of performing one's duty without attachment to the results. When devotees commit themselves to God, they naturally align their actions with dharma. This alignment fosters a life marked by righteousness, integrity, and ethical decision-making.

2. **Compassion and Service**: The practice of bhakti encourages selfless service (seva) to others. As devotees recognize the divine presence in all beings, they are inspired to act with compassion and kindness. The teachings of various saints, such as Tulsidas and Mirabai, emphasize the importance of serving humanity as a manifestation of devotion to God. This act of service not only fulfills a moral obligation but also strengthens the bonds of community and mutual respect.
3. **Detachment from Ego**: Selfless devotion helps to dissolve the ego, which is often the root cause of immoral behavior. When individuals focus on their relationship with God rather than personal gain, they cultivate humility and selflessness. The **Bhagavad Gita** teaches that true renunciation comes from dedicating one's actions to God, allowing individuals to rise above petty concerns and ego-driven desires.

Wealth: The Fruit of Righteous Action

The relationship between selfless devotion and material prosperity is intricately woven into Hindu thought. Bhakti is not viewed as a rejection of material wealth but rather as a means to achieve abundance through ethical living.

1. **Divine Blessings**: Many Hindu texts affirm that sincere devotion invites divine blessings.

The **Bhagavata Purana** recounts the stories of great devotees like Prahlada and Dhruva, whose unwavering faith and devotion led to immense material and spiritual rewards. This belief underscores the idea that God rewards those who surrender their lives to Him with both spiritual abundance and material prosperity.

2. **Right Action and Ethical Wealth**: Selfless devotion encourages individuals to pursue wealth through righteous means. The **Gita** emphasizes that performing one's duty without attachment to the results leads to true prosperity. By focusing on ethical actions, devotees create a foundation for wealth that is sustainable and fulfilling. This principle highlights that wealth acquired through moral means is ultimately more rewarding than wealth gained through deceit or exploitation.
3. **Generosity and Abundance**: The act of giving and sharing is integral to the bhakti tradition. Engaging in charitable acts as an expression of devotion not only enhances one's wealth but also fosters a sense of fulfilment that transcends material gain. The **Ramayana** illustrates how Lord Rama's generosity towards his subjects created a harmonious kingdom, reinforcing the belief that wealth is best utilized when shared for the greater good.

Amenities and Overall Well-Being

Selfless devotion extends beyond morality and wealth to encompass various dimensions of life, promoting holistic well-being.

1. **Mental Peace and Happiness**: The practice of bhakti brings inner peace and joy. By surrendering to God, devotees find solace and strength in the face of life's challenges. The **Gita** teaches that those who are devoted to God remain unaffected by external turmoil, cultivating a deep sense of contentment. This mental peace is vital for navigating the stresses of daily life, fostering resilience and emotional stability.
2. **Community and Connection**: Bhakti fosters a sense of belonging and community. Engaging in group worship or spiritual gatherings creates bonds among devotees, reinforcing social and emotional support. The sense of community that arises from shared devotion enhances one's quality of life, promoting mutual well-being and emotional health. Festivals and communal prayers become opportunities for collective joy and spiritual growth.
3. **Holistic Fulfillment**: Ultimately, selfless devotion integrates all aspects of life—spiritual, moral, and material. When one dedicates their actions and outcomes to God, they navigate life's complexities with grace.

The **Bhagavad Gita** emphasizes that those who live with such awareness experience holistic fulfillment, transcending the limitations of worldly desires. This fulfillment is not solely dependent on external achievements but is rooted in a profound inner peace that comes from living in accordance with one's values.

The Role of Saints and Devotees

Throughout history, many saints and devotees have exemplified the transformative power of bhakti. Their lives serve as inspirational models, illustrating how selfless devotion can lead to a fulfilling existence.

1. **Ramanuja**: A revered philosopher and theologian, Ramanuja emphasized the importance of devotion and surrender to God. His teachings highlight that true knowledge comes from love and devotion, encouraging followers to cultivate a personal relationship with the divine. His emphasis on community and service has inspired countless devotees to pursue a life of righteousness and compassion.
2. **Tulsidas**: The author of the **Ramcharitmanas**, Tulsidas dedicated his life to the worship of Lord Rama. Through his poetry, he conveyed the principles of bhakti, illustrating how devotion leads to moral living and social harmony. His life exemplifies the

idea that selfless devotion not only enriches the individual but also uplifts the community.

3. **Mirabai**: A prominent figure in the Bhakti movement, Mirabai's unwavering devotion to Lord Krishna transcended societal norms. Her songs and poetry express profound love and surrender to God, demonstrating that true fulfillment arises from a deep emotional connection with the divine. Mirabai's life is a testament to how devotion can empower individuals to live authentically and joyfully.

The Philosophical Underpinnings of Bhakti

To understand the depth of selfless devotion, we must explore the philosophical concepts that underpin it. Hindu philosophy presents various perspectives on the nature of God, the self, and the universe, all of which inform the practice of bhakti.

1. **The Nature of God**: In Hinduism, God is often conceived as both immanent and transcendent. The personal form of God (Saguna Brahman) invites devotees to engage emotionally, while the formless aspect (Nirguna Brahman) represents the ultimate reality beyond attributes. Bhakti allows individuals to relate to the divine in a personal way, fostering a deep sense of connection and intimacy.

2. **The Self and Liberation**: The concept of **Atman** (the individual soul) is central to Hindu philosophy. Selfless devotion helps individuals realize their true nature as one with the divine. The **Bhagavad Gita** teaches that through devotion, one can transcend the limitations of the ego and achieve liberation (moksha). This understanding fosters a sense of peace and fulfillment, as devotees recognize their innate connection to the divine.
3. **The Interconnectedness of All Beings**: Hindu philosophy emphasizes the interconnectedness of all life. By recognizing the divine presence in all beings, devotees cultivate compassion and empathy. This awareness fosters a sense of unity and harmony, reinforcing the idea that selfless devotion to God translates into a commitment to the well-being of all.

The Practice of Bhakti: Rituals and Devotion

The practice of bhakti encompasses a variety of rituals and expressions, each contributing to the fulfillment of devotees in different ways.

1. **Prayer and Mantra**: Devotees engage in prayer and the recitation of mantras as acts of devotion. These practices create a sacred space for connecting with the divine. The repetition of names and qualities of God serves to focus the mind and foster a sense of

peace, reinforcing the devotee's commitment to selfless love.
2. **Puja and Offerings**: Ritual worship (puja) involves making offerings to deities, expressing gratitude and love. This act reinforces the devotee's relationship with God and serves as a reminder of the blessings received. Puja fosters a sense of connection and reverence, enhancing the spiritual experience.
3. **Satsang and Community Worship**: Engaging in community worship (satsang) allows devotees to share their experiences and support one another on the spiritual path. This collective practice enhances feelings of belonging and reinforces the moral values derived from selfless devotion.

The Transformative Power of Selfless Devotion

As we explore the myriad ways in which selfless devotion impacts various aspects of life, it becomes clear that the transformative power of bhakti is profound.

1. **Inner Transformation**: Selfless devotion encourages individuals to undergo a deep inner transformation. As they cultivate love and surrender to God, their perspectives shift, leading to greater self-awareness and emotional resilience. This transformation

fosters a sense of fulfillment that is rooted in authenticity and purpose.
2. **Impact on Relationships**: The practice of bhakti enhances interpersonal relationships by promoting compassion, understanding, and forgiveness. When individuals embody the qualities of love and service derived from devotion, they contribute to healthier, more fulfilling relationships. The emphasis on connection and empathy fosters a sense of community and support.
3. **Holistic Success**: The integration of selfless devotion into daily life leads to a holistic sense of success. Rather than viewing success solely through the lens of material achievement, devotees recognize the importance of moral integrity, emotional well-being, and spiritual growth. This holistic approach to success creates a more balanced and fulfilling life.

Challenges on the Path of Devotion

While the path of bhakti offers immense rewards, it is not without challenges.

1. **Distractions and Temptations**: In a fast-paced world, distractions and temptations can hinder one's commitment to devotion. The allure of material success and societal pressures may divert attention from spiritual pursuits. Recognizing these challenges is

essential for maintaining focus on the path of bhakti.
2. **Doubt and Uncertainty**: Doubts about one's faith or the presence of God can arise, leading to moments of spiritual crisis. Navigating these doubts requires resilience and a recommitment to practices that foster connection with the divine.
3. **The Need for Guidance**: The journey of bhakti is often enhanced by the guidance of spiritual mentors or communities. The lack of support or mentorship can make it challenging for individuals to navigate their spiritual path. Seeking out communities and teachers can provide valuable encouragement and insight.

The Path of Selfless Devotion

In conclusion, selfless devotion to God is a powerful catalyst for fulfilment in terms of morality, wealth, and overall well-being. The teachings found in Hindu texts illuminate the transformative potential of bhakti, guiding individuals toward a life rich in meaning and purpose.

By aligning actions with dharma, cultivating compassion, and embracing the interconnectedness of all beings, devotees experience profound moral growth. The pursuit of wealth through ethical means, rooted in divine blessings, reinforces the idea that true prosperity arises from righteous living. Moreover, the holistic fulfilment achieved through bhakti promotes mental peace, community connection, and a sense of belonging.

The lives of saints and devotees throughout history serve as inspirational examples of how selfless devotion can lead to a fulfilling existence. Their teachings encourage us to embrace the path of bhakti, recognizing that through love, surrender, and service, we can cultivate a deeper connection with the divine and enrich our lives in every dimension.

Ultimately, the journey of selfless devotion invites each individual to explore their unique relationship with God, fostering a life that embodies the principles of love, integrity, and service. In doing so, we discover the profound truth that fulfilment is not merely a destination but a way of being—rooted in the sacred bond between the devotee and the divine. Through this journey, we may find our true purpose and experience the richness of life in its fullest expression.

Chapter 4:

Becoming More Articulate

The Importance of Articulation: A Reflection on Communication and Mental Health

Introduction

In today's increasingly complex and fast-paced world, the ability to articulate thoughts and feelings with clarity is essential. Articulation transcends mere speech; it encompasses the ability to convey ideas effectively, engage in meaningful discourse, and foster connection. The skill of being articulate profoundly influences one's mental health, shaping individual experiences and the dynamics of relationships and communities. This exploration delves into the significance of articulation and its deep connection to mental well-being.

The Nature of Articulation

Articulation, at its essence, is the act of expressing thoughts in a coherent and organized manner. It involves more than just the mechanical aspects of speech; it requires a thoughtful arrangement of words and concepts that enables effective communication. This skill necessitates a command of language, an understanding of context, and an awareness of one's audience. To articulate effectively is to bridge the often tenuous gap between our internal landscapes and the external world.

Language itself is a powerful tool, shaping our perception of reality and influencing our interactions with others. Through language, we construct our identities, express our emotions, and navigate the intricate social fabric of our lives. The words we choose carry immense weight; they can inspire, provoke, comfort, or alienate. In this regard, being articulate allows us to harness the power of language, creating connections that enrich our experiences and foster understanding.

The Importance of Being Articulate

Clarity of thought is one of the most significant benefits of being articulate. When individuals can express their ideas clearly, they demonstrate a deeper understanding of those concepts. This clarity is essential for effective problem-solving and decision-making. Without the ability to articulate thoughts, individuals may find themselves grappling with confusion and frustration, unable to convey their needs or navigate complex situations.

Moreover, the act of articulating thoughts helps to crystallize them. The process of verbal expression often leads to further reflection and refinement. As we vocalize our ideas, we can identify gaps in our understanding and confront cognitive biases. This introspection fosters intellectual growth and emotional maturity, empowering us to engage more deeply with the world around us.

Effective communication is also the bedrock of healthy relationships. Articulation facilitates connection, allowing individuals to share their experiences, thoughts, and emotions in meaningful ways. When we can express ourselves clearly, we invite others to engage with us. This engagement can enhance empathy and understanding, fostering deeper connections with friends, family, and colleagues.

In contrast, poor articulation can lead to misunderstandings and conflicts. When individuals struggle to express their thoughts or feelings, they may resort to frustration or withdrawal, which can strain relationships. The inability to communicate effectively often results in feelings of isolation, as others may misinterpret intentions or emotions. This disconnect can exacerbate mental health challenges, leading to a cycle of negative thoughts and feelings.

The Link Between Articulation and Mental Health

The relationship between articulation and mental health is profound. Mental health issues can impede one's ability to express thoughts and feelings, creating a barrier to effective communication. For instance, anxiety can manifest as difficulty in articulating one's thoughts, leading to a sense of being overwhelmed or misunderstood. In such cases, individuals may feel trapped within their own minds, unable to convey their struggles to others.

Conversely, the ability to articulate one's experiences can serve as a powerful coping mechanism. Expressing thoughts and feelings provides a means of processing emotions, allowing individuals to confront their challenges more effectively. Whether through conversation, writing, or other forms of expression, articulation can act as a release valve, alleviating the pressure that often accompanies mental health struggles.

Articulation also plays a critical role in fostering resilience. By expressing thoughts and feelings, individuals can gain insights into their emotions and experiences. This self-awareness can lead to healthier coping strategies and a greater capacity to navigate life's challenges. Engaging in open dialogue about one's mental health can help destigmatize these issues, promoting a culture of understanding and support.

Moreover, being articulate can empower individuals to advocate for themselves. Whether in personal relationships, at work, or within larger societal contexts, the ability to communicate effectively enhances one's capacity to express needs and assert boundaries. This empowerment is crucial for mental well-being, as it fosters a sense of agency and control over one's life.

The Practice of Articulation

To cultivate articulation, one must engage in deliberate practice. This involves actively seeking opportunities to express thoughts and feelings, whether through conversation, writing, or creative endeavors. Engaging in discussions with others, especially those who may challenge our viewpoints, can sharpen our ability to articulate ideas clearly. Such exchanges encourage us to think critically and refine our understanding of various topics.

Journaling is another powerful tool for enhancing articulation. By writing regularly, individuals can explore their thoughts and emotions in a safe space. This practice not only promotes clarity but also serves as a means of reflection. Over time, journaling can lead to improved self-awareness and a greater capacity to articulate complex feelings or ideas.

Moreover, public speaking and storytelling can be valuable exercises in articulation. Participating in workshops or joining organizations that focus on communication skills can enhance one's confidence and effectiveness in expressing ideas. These experiences can reduce anxiety associated with speaking in front of others, fostering a sense of mastery over one's voice.

In conclusion, the importance of being articulate cannot be overstated. It shapes our relationships, enhances our mental health, and empowers us to navigate the complexities of life with greater confidence. The ability to express thoughts and feelings clearly is a vital skill that fosters connection, understanding, and resilience.

As we cultivate our articulation skills, we not only enrich our own lives but also contribute to the well-being of those around us. In a world that often feels fragmented and chaotic, the power of clear communication can be a transformative force, bridging gaps and fostering a deeper sense of community. By embracing the practice of articulation, we can engage more meaningfully with ourselves and others, ultimately enhancing our collective mental health and resilience in the face of life's challenges.

The Double-Edged Sword of Articulation: Why Being Articulate Can Be a Curse

Introduction

The ability to articulate thoughts and feelings is often heralded as a vital skill for success in personal and professional realms. Clarity in communication can lead to deeper connections, improved relationships, and enhanced self-expression. However, this very gift can also become a curse, laden with expectations, pressures, and emotional burdens. In this exploration, we will delve into the complexities of being articulate, examining how it can lead to misunderstandings, alienation, and psychological distress.

The Weight of Expectations

Being articulate often comes with high expectations from oneself and others. People may assume that those who can express themselves well are also equipped to handle complex situations and challenging conversations. This can create a pressure to always perform at a high level, leaving little room for vulnerability or error.

When articulate individuals struggle to convey their thoughts in certain situations, they may feel a heightened sense of failure. The discrepancy between their perceived ability and their actual experience can lead to self-doubt and frustration. This burden becomes even heavier in environments where communication is consistently scrutinized, such as workplaces or academic settings.

Moreover, being articulate can result in a lack of empathy from others. People may see articulate individuals as having it all together, failing to recognize the struggles and complexities behind their words. This can lead to feelings of isolation, as others may overlook the emotional nuances that articulate individuals experience. The expectation to always articulate oneself well can thus hinder authentic connection and support.

Misunderstandings and Misinterpretations

Another challenge of being articulate is the potential for misunderstandings and misinterpretations. While clarity is often the goal, the complexity of language can sometimes create confusion. Articulate individuals may use nuanced vocabulary or complex sentence structures, which can alienate those who do not share the same linguistic background or understanding.

In these instances, the very skill that should enhance communication can lead to a breakdown in understanding. What was meant to be a clear expression of thought may instead come across as pretentious or inaccessible. This can foster resentment or defensiveness in conversations, further complicating relationships.

Additionally, articulate individuals may find themselves overthinking their words. The desire to choose the "right" expression can lead to paralysis by analysis, where the fear of being misunderstood inhibits genuine expression. This internal conflict can generate anxiety, as individuals grapple with the need for clarity and the fear of miscommunication.

The Burden of Emotional Labor

Articulate individuals often engage in a significant amount of emotional labor. The ability to express oneself clearly requires a level of self-awareness and introspection that can be exhausting. Articulating complex feelings necessitates digging deep into one's emotional landscape, which can lead to emotional fatigue.

In conversations where emotions run high, articulate individuals may find themselves playing the role of mediator, striving to clarify misunderstandings and bridge gaps in communication. This can be particularly challenging in personal relationships, where the stakes are often higher and emotions are more intense. The responsibility to articulate thoughts and feelings for both oneself and others can create a sense of burden that weighs heavily on the individual.

Furthermore, the emotional toll of articulation can lead to burnout. When articulate individuals consistently find themselves in positions where they must navigate complex emotional landscapes—whether in friendships, family dynamics, or professional environments—they may eventually feel drained. The constant demand to communicate effectively can deplete their emotional reserves, leaving them feeling overwhelmed and exhausted.

The Paradox of Vulnerability

Being articulate can paradoxically diminish the space for vulnerability. While clear communication is often celebrated as a strength, it can also create a façade of invulnerability. Articulate individuals may feel pressure to present themselves as composed and self-assured, leaving little room for authentic expressions of vulnerability.

In many cultures, vulnerability is often viewed as a weakness. This societal bias can lead articulate individuals to suppress their genuine feelings, fearing that vulnerability will undermine their perceived competence. The result is a disconnection between their internal emotional experiences and their outward expressions, creating a chasm that can foster feelings of loneliness and isolation.

Moreover, the pressure to articulate thoughts can inhibit the exploration of messy, complex emotions. Articulate individuals may struggle to navigate feelings that are difficult to express in precise terms, leading to a sense of frustration and alienation from their own emotional experiences. The inability to articulate vulnerability can further reinforce the perception that articulate individuals are emotionally distant or inaccessible.

The Isolation of Articulation

Articulation can create a sense of isolation, particularly when one's communication style is misaligned with that of others. Articulate individuals may find themselves in environments where their clarity and precision set them apart, leading to feelings of alienation. The very skill that enables effective communication can also create a barrier between individuals.

In social settings, articulate individuals may feel like outsiders, struggling to connect with those who do not share their linguistic proficiency or intellectual curiosity. This can be especially pronounced in groups where informal language and colloquialisms are the norm. The resulting disconnection can foster feelings of loneliness, as articulate individuals grapple with the desire to connect while facing barriers to understanding.

Furthermore, the pressure to maintain articulate communication can lead to a sense of performance anxiety. The fear of not meeting expectations can inhibit genuine expression, making it difficult to engage authentically with others. This performance-oriented mindset can create a cycle of isolation, as articulate individuals retreat into themselves rather than risk vulnerability in communication.

Navigating the Curse

Recognizing the potential curses of articulation is essential for fostering a healthier relationship with communication. Articulate individuals can benefit from strategies that promote balance and authenticity in their interactions.

First, cultivating self-compassion is vital. Recognizing that everyone struggles with communication at times can alleviate the pressure to always perform at a high level. Embracing imperfection allows individuals to express themselves more freely, creating space for vulnerability and authenticity in their interactions.

Second, developing emotional awareness can enhance communication. By tuning into their own emotional experiences, articulate individuals can better navigate the complexities of their feelings. This self-awareness can lead to more genuine expressions of vulnerability, fostering deeper connections with others.

Finally, practising active listening can bridge the gap between articulate individuals and those who may struggle with communication. By prioritizing understanding over articulation, individuals can create a more inclusive and empathetic dialogue. This shift in focus can foster authentic connections and diminish feelings of isolation.

While being articulate is often celebrated as a strength, it can also carry significant burdens. The weight of expectations, the risk of misunderstandings, the emotional labour involved, and the paradox of vulnerability all contribute to the complexities of articulation.

Recognizing the potential curses of this skill is essential for fostering a balanced and healthy relationship with communication. By cultivating self-compassion, emotional awareness, and active listening, articulate individuals can navigate the challenges of communication more effectively, creating deeper connections and enriching their experiences. Ultimately, articulation is a powerful tool, but like any tool, it requires mindfulness and care in its use.

Breaking the curse of being articulate involves embracing vulnerability, fostering authentic connections, and developing strategies to navigate communication challenges. Here are some key approaches to consider:

1. Embrace Imperfection

Understanding the Nature of Imperfection

Embracing imperfection involves recognizing that no one communicates flawlessly. Misunderstandings are a natural part of human interaction. Accepting that you will sometimes misspeak or fail to convey your thoughts as intended can relieve the pressure that often accompanies articulate communication.

Benefits of Embracing Imperfection

By allowing yourself to be imperfect, you create an environment where authentic communication can thrive. You foster a sense of freedom that encourages experimentation with language and expression. This mindset can lead to more honest conversations, as you may feel less inhibited about sharing your true feelings and thoughts.

Practical Steps to Embrace Imperfection

1. **Reframe Your Thoughts**: Shift your perspective on mistakes. Instead of viewing them as failures, see them as opportunities for growth and learning.
2. **Practice Self-Acceptance**: Acknowledge that everyone has strengths and weaknesses. Accepting your flaws as part of being human can help alleviate the burden of perfectionism.
3. **Engage in Open Conversations**: Discuss the concept of imperfection with trusted friends. Sharing your struggles can create a supportive environment where others feel encouraged to do the same.

2. Cultivate Self-Compassion

Understanding Self-Compassion

Self-compassion involves treating yourself with kindness during difficult moments. It requires acknowledging your feelings without judgment and recognizing that suffering is part of the human experience.

The Importance of Self-Compassion in Communication

When you practice self-compassion, you reduce the harsh inner critic that often emerges when you struggle to articulate your thoughts. This supportive mindset allows for greater emotional resilience, helping you navigate challenging conversations with more ease.

Strategies to Cultivate Self-Compassion

1. **Mindfulness Practices**: Engage in mindfulness meditation to become more aware of your thoughts and feelings without judgment. This practice can help you observe your internal dialogue and cultivate a kinder approach to yourself.
2. **Positive Self-Talk**: Replace negative self-talk with affirmations and compassionate statements. Remind yourself that it's okay to struggle and that you are doing your best.
3. **Connect with Others**: Share your experiences of self-compassion with friends or support groups. Hearing others' stories can reinforce the idea that you are not alone in your struggles.

3. Prioritize Active Listening

The Essence of Active Listening

Active listening is a communication technique that involves fully focusing on the speaker, understanding their message, and responding thoughtfully. It requires not just hearing words but engaging with the emotions and intentions behind them.

Benefits of Active Listening

By prioritizing active listening, you create a more empathetic environment. This approach can foster deeper connections, as it demonstrates respect for the speaker's thoughts and feelings. When others feel heard, they are more likely to respond in kind, leading to richer, more meaningful conversations.

Techniques for Practicing Active Listening

1. **Maintain Eye Contact**: Show that you are engaged by making eye contact and nodding to indicate understanding.
2. **Avoid Interrupting**: Let the speaker finish their thoughts without interruption. Resist the urge to formulate your response while they are speaking.
3. **Ask Clarifying Questions**: Encourage deeper conversation by asking open-ended questions that invite the speaker to elaborate on their thoughts.

4. Share Vulnerabilities

The Power of Vulnerability

Vulnerability involves exposing your true self, including fears, uncertainties, and imperfections.

Sharing vulnerabilities can foster trust and intimacy in relationships, allowing for deeper connections.

Why Sharing Vulnerabilities Matters

When you openly share your struggles, it normalizes the experience of imperfection. It allows others to feel safe doing the same, creating an atmosphere of authenticity. This mutual openness can lead to richer dialogues and a greater sense of community.

Ways to Share Vulnerabilities

1. **Choose the Right Setting**: Find a comfortable environment where you feel safe expressing yourself. This can be with close friends, family, or support groups.
2. **Use "I" Statements**: Frame your experiences in a personal context. For example, "I feel overwhelmed when..." This approach emphasizes your feelings without placing blame on others.
3. **Be Open to Responses**: When you share vulnerabilities, be receptive to how others respond. Their empathy can reinforce the strength of your connection.

5. Simplify Your Language

The Importance of Simplicity in Communication

Simplifying your language involves expressing thoughts in a clear and accessible manner. This practice can make conversations more inclusive and engaging, allowing for a broader audience to connect with your ideas.

Benefits of Using Simple Language

When you simplify your language, you lower barriers to understanding. This inclusivity fosters connection, as it allows others to engage with your thoughts without feeling intimidated by complexity.

Strategies to Simplify Language

1. **Know Your Audience**: Tailor your language to your audience. Consider their background, knowledge level, and familiarity with the topic.
2. **Use Everyday Vocabulary**: Opt for common words and phrases over jargon or complex terminology. This practice can enhance clarity and engagement.
3. **Be Concise**: Strive for brevity. Communicating your ideas in fewer words can often enhance understanding and retention.

6. Reflect on Emotional Experiences

The Role of Reflection in Communication

Reflecting on your emotional experiences involves taking time to process and understand your feelings. This self-awareness can enhance your ability to articulate thoughts clearly and authentically.

Benefits of Emotional Reflection

By engaging in reflection, you gain insights into your emotional landscape. This clarity can lead to more genuine expressions of your feelings, reducing the likelihood of misunderstandings.

Techniques for Reflective Practice

1. **Journaling**: Write about your thoughts and feelings regularly. This practice can help you clarify your emotions and identify patterns in your experiences.
2. **Creative Expression**: Engage in artistic activities that allow you to express your feelings. This can be through art, music, or writing, providing a safe outlet for emotions.
3. **Mind Mapping**: Use visual tools to map out your emotions and thoughts. This can help you organize complex feelings and articulate them more clearly.

7. Practice Mindfulness

Understanding Mindfulness

Mindfulness is the practice of being present in the moment, fully aware of your thoughts and feelings without judgment. This approach can help reduce anxiety and improve your capacity for clear communication.

Benefits of Mindfulness in Articulation

By practicing mindfulness, you become more attuned to your emotional state. This awareness can enhance your ability to express yourself without the weight of overthinking or fear of judgment.

Mindfulness Techniques

1. **Meditation**: Dedicate time each day to meditate. Focus on your breath and observe your thoughts as they arise, allowing them to pass without attachment.
2. **Grounding Exercises**: Engage in grounding techniques, such as focusing on your senses. Notice the sounds, sights, and sensations around you to anchor yourself in the present moment.
3. **Mindful Communication**: Practice being fully present in conversations. Focus on the speaker and your own feelings, allowing for genuine engagement.

8. Seek Feedback

The Importance of Feedback in Communication

Seeking feedback involves asking others for their perspectives on your communication style. Constructive feedback can enhance your articulation skills and promote personal growth.

Benefits of Receiving Feedback

Feedback provides valuable insights into how your communication is perceived. This understanding can help you identify areas for improvement and bolster your confidence in expressing yourself.

Strategies for Seeking Feedback

1. **Choose Trusted Individuals**: Approach friends, family, or colleagues whom you trust to provide honest and supportive feedback.
2. **Ask Specific Questions**: Inquire about specific aspects of your communication, such as clarity, tone, or engagement. This can lead to more actionable insights.
3. **Be Open to Critique**: Approach feedback with an open mind. Recognize that constructive criticism is an opportunity for growth, not a personal attack.

9. Create a Supportive Environment

The Role of a Supportive Environment

A supportive environment fosters open communication and authentic expression.

Surrounding yourself with individuals who value vulnerability and empathy can enhance your ability to articulate thoughts and feelings.

Benefits of a Supportive Community

When you feel supported, you are more likely to take risks in communication. This sense of security can lead to deeper connections and a greater willingness to share vulnerabilities.

Ways to Build a Supportive Environment

1. **Engage in Meaningful Conversations**: Initiate discussions that encourage openness and authenticity. Create a space where everyone feels comfortable sharing.
2. **Model Vulnerability**: Lead by example. Share your own experiences and feelings to encourage others to do the same.
3. **Establish Trust**: Build trust within your community by actively listening, respecting boundaries, and being nonjudgmental.

10. Reframe Your Perspective

The Importance of Perspective in Communication

Reframing your perspective involves shifting how you view articulation. Instead of seeing it solely as a skill, recognize it as one of many ways to connect with others.

Benefits of a Broader Perspective

By broadening your perspective, you reduce the pressure associated with articulation. This shift allows you to prioritize emotional resonance and understanding over the need for precise language.

Strategies for Reframing Perspective

1. **Reflect on Your Values**: Consider what truly matters in communication. Emphasize connection, empathy, and understanding over perfection.
2. **Engage in Diverse Conversations**: Seek out discussions with individuals from different backgrounds or experiences. This exposure can broaden your understanding of communication and foster empathy.
3. **Challenge Negative Beliefs**: Identify any limiting beliefs you hold about your communication abilities. Work to reframe these beliefs into more empowering narratives.
4. Being articulate, much like any skill, is enriched by the presence of role models who inspire and guide us. Here are some of my favourites and the invaluable lessons I have gleaned from them.

Being articulate, much like any skill, is enriched by the presence of role models who inspire and guide us. Here are some of my favourites and the invaluable lessons I have gleaned from them.

Jordan Peterson: Clarity and Structure

Overview of Communication Style

Jordan Peterson is renowned for his articulate and structured communication, particularly in the realm of psychology, philosophy, and social commentary. His ability to convey complex ideas in a clear, accessible manner has garnered him a substantial following. He often employs a logical framework, using well-defined concepts and examples to illustrate his points.

Key Lessons

1. **Clarity of Thought**
   - **Conceptual Precision:** Peterson emphasizes the importance of understanding and clearly defining concepts before discussing them. This involves breaking down complex ideas into simpler components, ensuring that both the speaker and the audience share a common understanding.
   - **Application:** When articulating your thoughts, take time to define key terms and ideas. This practice can prevent misunderstandings and create a solid foundation for discussion.

2. **Structured Argumentation**
    - **Logical Flow:** Peterson often organizes his arguments in a logical sequence, guiding the audience through his thought process. This structure helps listeners follow along and grasp the nuances of his arguments.
    - **Application:** Use outlines or bullet points when preparing for discussions or presentations. Organizing your thoughts beforehand can lead to a more coherent delivery.
3. **Engagement with the Audience**
    - **Interactive Dialogue:** Peterson frequently engages with his audience, encouraging questions and discussion. This approach fosters a sense of connection and allows for deeper exploration of topics.
    - **Application:** Encourage feedback and questions during conversations. This can create a more dynamic exchange and help clarify any points of confusion.
4. **Narrative and Storytelling**
    - **Personal Anecdotes:** Peterson often shares personal stories and experiences to illustrate his points. This technique not only makes his arguments relatable but also enhances emotional engagement.
    - **Application:** Incorporate personal stories or relevant anecdotes in your

communication. This can help make your message more memorable and impactful.

S. Jaishankar: Diplomatic Nuance

Overview of Communication Style

S. Jaishankar, India's External Affairs Minister, exemplifies the art of diplomatic communication. His style is characterized by nuance, respect, and an understanding of the complexities of international relations. He balances assertiveness with a keen awareness of different perspectives.

Key Lessons

1. **Contextual Awareness**
   - **Understanding Nuances:** Jaishankar's communication reflects a deep understanding of the cultural and political contexts in which he operates. He tailors his messages to suit the audience and the situation.
   - **Application:** When communicating, consider the cultural and contextual factors that may influence how your message is received. This can enhance your effectiveness and prevent miscommunication.
2. **Empathy and Respect**

- **Building Relationships:** Jaishankar emphasizes the importance of empathy in diplomacy. He listens carefully to others' viewpoints, fostering mutual respect and understanding.
- **Application:** Practice active listening in conversations. Show genuine interest in others' perspectives to build rapport and create a more collaborative environment.

3. **Strategic Communication**
   - **Choosing Words Wisely:** Jaishankar is adept at choosing his words carefully, especially in sensitive situations. His strategic use of language helps convey strength without alienating others.
   - **Application:** Think critically about the language you use. Avoid inflammatory or ambiguous terms, and instead opt for words that promote dialogue and understanding.

4. **Long-Term Vision**
   - **Beyond the Immediate:** Jaishankar often considers the long-term implications of communication in diplomacy. He understands that words can shape relationships and influence future interactions.
   - **Application:** Be mindful of the long-term effects of your communication. Consider how your words may impact

relationships and your reputation over time.

J. Sai Deepak: Advocacy Through Persuasion

Overview of Communication Style

J. Sai Deepak is a lawyer, author, and public speaker known for his passionate advocacy and articulate expression. His communication style is marked by a blend of legal reasoning and cultural insights, often framed within a philosophical context.

Key Lessons

1. **Persuasive Rhetoric**
    - **Building Arguments:** Deepak employs a variety of rhetorical techniques to persuade his audience, including logical reasoning, emotional appeals, and ethical considerations. His ability to weave these elements together makes his arguments compelling.
    - **Application:** Use rhetorical techniques to enhance your arguments. Incorporate logic, emotion, and ethical appeals to engage your audience more deeply.
2. **Cultural Context**
    - **Rooting Arguments in Culture:** Deepak often grounds his discussions in cultural and historical contexts, making his points resonate more with his audience. This

connection to culture enhances the relevance of his arguments.
- **Application:** Consider the cultural and historical context when discussing your ideas. Relating your arguments to familiar narratives can make them more relatable and impactful.

3. **Storytelling as a Tool**
   - **Engaging Narratives:** Deepak effectively uses storytelling to illustrate complex legal and philosophical concepts. This technique not only clarifies his points but also captivates his audience.
   - **Application:** Incorporate storytelling into your communication. Share narratives that relate to your message to enhance engagement and understanding.

4. **Authenticity in Advocacy**
   - **Staying True to Values:** Deepak emphasizes the importance of authenticity in advocacy. He communicates his beliefs passionately, drawing from personal conviction and integrity.
   - **Application:** Be authentic in your communication. Speak from your values and experiences to create a more genuine connection with your audience.

Plato: Philosophical Dialogue

Overview of Communication Style

Plato, the ancient philosopher, is renowned for his dialectical method, particularly through dialogues featuring Socratic questioning. His style emphasizes inquiry, exploration, and the pursuit of truth through conversation.

Key Lessons

1. **The Socratic Method**
    - **Asking Questions:** Plato's dialogues often employ the Socratic method, which involves asking probing questions to stimulate critical thinking and illuminate ideas. This technique encourages deep exploration of topics.
    - **Application:** Use questions as a tool for engagement. Encourage others to think critically by asking open-ended questions that prompt reflection.
2. **Dialogue Over Monologue**
    - **Collaborative Exploration:** Plato's style emphasizes dialogue as a means of discovering truth collectively. This approach fosters collaboration and respect for diverse perspectives.
    - **Application:** Engage in conversations as a collaborative process. Encourage input and discussion rather than dominating the conversation with monologues.
3. **Exploring Complex Ideas**
    - **Delving into Philosophy:** Plato's dialogues tackle profound philosophical concepts,

often requiring nuanced exploration. This method highlights the importance of depth in communication.
- **Application:** Don't shy away from complexity. Be willing to explore challenging ideas and encourage thoughtful discourse around them.

4. **Critical Thinking**
   - **Challenging Assumptions:** Plato encourages questioning assumptions and beliefs. This critical approach fosters deeper understanding and intellectual growth.
   - **Application:** Promote critical thinking in discussions. Encourage yourself and others to question preconceived notions and explore alternative viewpoints.

Marcus Aurelius: Stoic Wisdom

Overview of Communication Style

Marcus Aurelius, the Stoic philosopher and Roman Emperor, is known for his reflective writings in "Meditations." His style emphasizes introspection, self-discipline, and the importance of perspective in communication.

Key Lessons

1. **Self-Reflection**
   - **Understanding Oneself:** Aurelius advocates for self-reflection as a means of

understanding one's thoughts and emotions. This introspection informs how he communicates with others.
    - **Application:** Engage in regular self-reflection to understand your emotions and motivations. This awareness can enhance your communication by grounding it in authenticity.
2. **Calmness and Composure**
    - **Staying Calm Under Pressure:** Aurelius emphasizes the importance of maintaining composure, even in challenging situations. His calm demeanour fosters clarity and thoughtful communication.
    - **Application:** Practice techniques to manage stress and maintain calmness during conversations. This can help you articulate your thoughts more clearly and effectively.
3. **Perspective-Taking**
    - **Understanding Others:** Aurelius emphasizes the importance of empathy and understanding others' perspectives. This approach fosters compassionate communication.
    - **Application:** Actively seek to understand the viewpoints of others. This practice can enhance your ability to articulate responses that resonate with their concerns.
4. **Principles Over Emotions**
    - **Guided by Values:** Aurelius emphasizes living in accordance with one's principles rather than being swayed by emotions. This

approach can lead to more thoughtful and deliberate communication.
- **Application:** Ground your communication in your values and principles. This can enhance your credibility and strengthen your message.

Om Swami: Spiritual Insight

Overview of Communication Style

Om Swami is a contemporary spiritual teacher known for his insights on spirituality, mindfulness, and self-awareness. His communication style blends wisdom with a compassionate, approachable demeanor.

Key Lessons

1. **Mindfulness in Communication**
   - **Being Present:** Om Swami emphasizes mindfulness in every aspect of life, including communication. Being fully present enhances the quality of interactions.
   - **Application:** Practice mindfulness techniques to remain present during conversations. This can help you listen actively and respond thoughtfully.
2. **Compassionate Communication**
   - **Empathy and Kindness:** Om Swami advocates for compassion in communication, emphasizing the

importance of kindness and understanding.
- **Application:** Approach conversations with empathy. Consider others' feelings and perspectives, fostering a supportive atmosphere.

3. **Simplicity and Clarity**
   - **Clear Messaging:** Om Swami often communicates profound ideas in simple, accessible language. This clarity makes his teachings relatable and easy to understand.
   - **Application:** Strive for simplicity in your language. Avoid jargon and complex terminology, focusing instead on clear, relatable expressions.

4. **Holistic Perspective**
   - **Integrating Mind, Body, and Spirit:** Om Swami emphasizes the interconnectedness of mind, body, and spirit. This holistic view informs his approach to communication and relationships.
   - **Application:** Consider the whole person in your interactions. Recognize the emotional, physical, and spiritual dimensions of communication.

Through the exploration of these figures—Jordan Peterson, S. Jaishankar, J. Sai Deepak, Plato, Marcus Aurelius, and Om Swami—we gain profound insights into the art of articulation. Each individual brings unique perspectives and techniques, emphasizing the importance of clarity, empathy, cultural context, critical thinking, and mindfulness in effective communication. By integrating these lessons into our own communication practices, we can enhance our ability to connect meaningfully with others and articulate our thoughts with authenticity and impact.

Part I:
Using the Pen

Writing as a Tool for Psychological Improvement and Cognitive Enhancement

Introduction

Writing transcends mere communication; it serves as a profound medium for personal exploration and cognitive development. Influential thinkers such as Jordan Peterson, Marcus Aurelius, and Seneca have recognized the transformative power of writing in enhancing psychological thinking and stimulating brain activity. By examining their insights, we can appreciate how writing can become an essential practice for self-discovery, emotional regulation, and intellectual growth.

The Philosophical Foundation of Writing

Jordan Peterson: The Search for Meaning

Jordan Peterson emphasizes the importance of meaning in life. He suggests that articulating our thoughts through writing can clarify our beliefs and values. By confronting our inner dialogues and documenting them, we create a structure that enables us to evaluate our motivations and decisions critically. This process of articulation allows us to recognize cognitive biases and irrational fears, leading to more informed choices.

Peterson encourages individuals to write daily, emphasizing that this practice can illuminate the dark corners of our psyche. When we express our thoughts on paper, we externalize them, making it easier to confront and analyze our emotions and experiences. This act of translation transforms vague feelings into coherent narratives, facilitating psychological growth.

Stoicism: Seneca's Reflection on Writing

Seneca, a Stoic philosopher, regarded writing as a means to achieve clarity and virtue. In his letters, he advises self-examination through reflection. Writing enables individuals to confront their thoughts and emotions candidly, fostering self-awareness. Seneca believed that by documenting our experiences, we gain insight into our reactions and can cultivate emotional resilience.

For Seneca, the written word serves as a mirror, reflecting our inner turmoil and desires. This reflection allows us to evaluate our values and align our actions accordingly. By engaging in this practice, we learn to navigate life's challenges with wisdom and fortitude, ultimately enhancing our psychological well-being.

Marcus Aurelius: Journaling as a Practice of Self-Discipline

Marcus Aurelius used journaling as a method for self-discipline and contemplation. His "Meditations" reveal how writing provided him with a framework for processing his thoughts and emotions. Aurelius's reflections illustrate the Stoic belief that by examining our inner lives, we can cultivate virtues like courage, patience, and humility.

Aurelius's writing was not merely an expression of his thoughts; it was a disciplined practice aimed at personal improvement. Through his journal, he confronted the chaos of existence, striving to maintain a rational perspective amidst life's challenges. This disciplined approach to writing allows individuals to cultivate a sense of purpose and clarity, reinforcing their psychological resilience.

The Cognitive Benefits of Writing

Engaging the Brain: Neuroscientific Insights

Research from the National Institutes of Health (NIH) highlights the cognitive benefits of writing, particularly in enhancing brain activity. Writing engages multiple brain regions, including those responsible for emotional processing, memory, and critical thinking. This engagement promotes neuroplasticity, allowing the brain to reorganize itself and form new connections.

When we write, especially in expressive forms, we stimulate areas associated with emotional regulation. This activation enhances our ability to process complex emotions and facilitates better decision-making. Writing also reinforces memory, as the act of committing thoughts to paper helps solidify information in our minds.

Writing Techniques for Psychological Improvement

Journaling for Self-Discovery

Journaling serves as a powerful tool for self-discovery. By regularly documenting our thoughts and feelings, we cultivate self-awareness and clarity. This practice can take various forms, including daily reflections, gratitude journaling, and goal setting.

1. **Daily Reflection**: Setting aside time each day to reflect on experiences and emotions encourages a deeper understanding of oneself. This ritual fosters mindfulness and helps individuals identify patterns in their behavior.
2. **Gratitude Journaling**: Writing about what we are grateful for shifts focus from negativity to positivity, enhancing overall mental well-being. This practice promotes a sense of

appreciation and helps mitigate feelings of anxiety and depression.
3. **Goal Setting**: Using a journal to articulate goals and strategies fosters clarity and motivation. This process allows individuals to break down complex aspirations into manageable steps, reinforcing a sense of purpose.

Creative Writing: Exploring Emotions

Creative writing serves as an emotional outlet, allowing individuals to explore complex feelings and experiences in a safe space. Through poetry, fiction, or personal essays, we can navigate our emotional landscapes and cultivate empathy.

1. **Character Exploration**: Writing from the perspective of different characters fosters empathy and understanding of diverse human experiences. This practice encourages writers to step outside their own narratives, enhancing emotional intelligence.
2. **Stream of Consciousness**: Engaging in free writing without concern for structure unlocks subconscious thoughts and feelings. This can lead to deeper self-awareness and an authentic expression of emotions.

Academic Writing: Fostering Critical Thinking

Academic writing challenges individuals to engage critically with ideas and articulate arguments clearly. This practice enhances analytical skills and promotes a deeper understanding of complex subjects.

1. **Literature Reviews**: Writing literature reviews compels writers to engage critically with existing knowledge, identify gaps, and formulate their ideas. This process reinforces the importance of evidence-based reasoning.
2. **Argumentative Essays**: Crafting essays that present a specific position enhances the ability to construct logical arguments and consider opposing viewpoints. This practice is invaluable in developing critical thinking skills.

Establishing a Writing Routine

Creating a Dedicated Space for Writing

To fully benefit from writing, it is essential to establish a consistent writing routine. Creating a dedicated space for writing helps foster focus and creativity. This physical separation allows for a deeper engagement with the writing process.

1. **Eliminate Distractions**: Reducing distractions during writing sessions cultivates a state of concentration. Turning off

notifications and setting boundaries can enhance focus and productivity.
2. **Setting a Schedule**: Allocating specific times for writing creates a sense of accountability and commitment. Consistency reinforces the habit, making writing a regular part of life.
3. **Using Prompts**: If writer's block arises, prompts can serve as a helpful starting point. They can provide structure and direction, encouraging exploration of new ideas.

The Connection Between Writing and Mental Health

Therapeutic Writing

Therapeutic writing has emerged as a valuable tool in mental health treatment. Expressive writing has been shown to reduce symptoms of anxiety and depression by allowing individuals to process traumatic experiences and emotional distress.

1. **Cognitive Behavioral Writing**: Writing about negative thoughts and challenging them can facilitate cognitive restructuring. This technique helps individuals reframe their perspectives and develop healthier thought patterns.
2. **Letter Writing**: Composing letters to oneself or others, even if never sent, can promote emotional closure and self-exploration. This

practice provides a safe outlet for expressing unresolved feelings.

The interplay between writing, psychological improvement, and cognitive enhancement is profound. By drawing on the insights of thinkers like Jordan Peterson, Marcus Aurelius, and Seneca, we see that writing is more than a tool for communication; it is a means of self-discovery, emotional regulation, and intellectual growth.

Incorporating writing into our daily lives can lead to significant improvements in mental well-being, critical thinking, and overall cognitive functioning. By engaging in practices like journaling, creative writing, and academic exploration, we can unlock the transformative potential of our thoughts, fostering deeper understanding and personal growth. Writing is not merely an act of creation; it is an act of reflection, clarity, and ultimately, empowerment.

The Influence of Writing on Personality Development

Writing is often seen as a tool for communication, a means of expressing thoughts and ideas. However, its impact on the human experience runs much deeper, shaping our identities and influencing our personalities in profound ways. The relationship between writing and personality is intricate, involving emotional exploration, cognitive processing, and self-reflection. Through various forms of writing, individuals not only convey their experiences but also construct and reconstruct their understanding of themselves and the world around them.

At its core, personality consists of enduring patterns of thoughts, feelings, and behaviors that define who we are. It encompasses a range of traits, from how we interact with others to how we cope with stress. Psychologists often describe personality through frameworks like the Big Five personality traits—openness, conscientiousness, extraversion, agreeableness, and neuroticism. Each of these traits can be influenced and shaped by writing practices, which serve as a reflective canvas where individuals can articulate their thoughts and feelings.

Writing acts as a mirror that reflects our internal landscapes. When we write, we engage in a form of self-dialogue that encourages introspection. This self-examination fosters greater self-awareness, allowing us to recognize our thoughts, emotions, and motivations. As we articulate our experiences on paper, we begin to see patterns in our behavior, illuminating the aspects of our personality that we may not have consciously acknowledged. This awareness is the first step toward personal growth, as it enables us to challenge and reshape our self-concept.

One of the most powerful forms of writing for personality development is journaling. Journaling serves as a space for emotional exploration and cognitive processing. It allows individuals to document their daily experiences, thoughts, and feelings, providing a narrative thread that connects their past, present, and future. This continuous act of writing helps clarify emotions, especially in times of distress. By externalizing thoughts, individuals can gain perspective, which often leads to insights about their emotional responses and coping mechanisms.

Through journaling, people can engage in emotional regulation. Writing about intense feelings can transform those emotions from chaotic internal experiences into structured narratives. This shift is crucial, as it fosters resilience. When individuals write about their struggles and triumphs, they learn to navigate challenges with a greater sense of clarity and control. This practice not only enhances emotional intelligence but also builds character, as individuals learn to embrace vulnerability and authenticity.

Moreover, journaling allows for identity exploration. Individuals often grapple with questions about who they are and what they stand for. Writing serves as a tool for examining these questions, encouraging a deeper understanding of personal values and beliefs. As individuals articulate their thoughts on paper, they may find that their views evolve over time. This evolution is an essential aspect of personality development, as it reflects the dynamic nature of identity. By documenting their journey, individuals can trace how their experiences and reflections contribute to the ongoing formation of their self-concept.

Creative writing also plays a significant role in shaping personality. Engaging in storytelling, poetry, or fiction allows individuals to explore different facets of their identity. Through creative writing, they can experiment with diverse perspectives, motivations, and emotional responses. This exploration enhances empathy and understanding, as writers often find themselves stepping into the shoes of their characters, grappling with their dilemmas and joys. This imaginative process not only enriches their emotional repertoire but also fosters a more nuanced understanding of human experience.

The act of creating fictional worlds encourages writers to reflect on their values and beliefs. Characters often embody traits that resonate with the writer's own personality or serve as a counterpoint to their self-image. This exploration can lead to insights about one's strengths and weaknesses, allowing for a more integrated sense of self. Through the lens of fiction, individuals can confront their fears, desires, and aspirations in a safe and structured manner, leading to transformative realizations that can influence their real-world interactions.

Moreover, academic writing also contributes to personality development, albeit in a different manner. Writing essays, research papers, and critical analyses encourages individuals to engage deeply with ideas and concepts. This engagement fosters critical thinking, as writers must articulate arguments, analyze evidence, and synthesize information. The process of structuring complex ideas on paper enhances cognitive flexibility and encourages a more organized thought process. As individuals grapple with new information and perspectives, they may find that their beliefs and attitudes shift, reflecting a growing openness to new ideas—a trait associated with a more expansive personality.

Writing also serves as a tool for advocacy and self-assertion. When individuals write about social issues or personal experiences, they often engage in a process of empowerment. Writing can be a way to assert one's voice in a world that may feel overwhelming or silencing. This act of self-expression fosters a sense of agency, as individuals recognize their ability to influence their surroundings through their words. The courage to share personal stories or advocate for social change not only strengthens their identity but also reinforces traits such as assertiveness and confidence.

Furthermore, writing in collaborative settings, such as workshops or group projects, can significantly impact personality development. Interacting with others in these contexts encourages individuals to share their thoughts and receive feedback. This exchange fosters a sense of community and belonging, which can be essential for personal growth. Collaborative writing experiences promote social skills, adaptability, and openness, as individuals learn to navigate differing perspectives and negotiate ideas.

The digital age has transformed the landscape of writing, introducing new platforms and forms of expression. Social media, blogs, and online forums provide individuals with opportunities to share their thoughts and experiences with a global audience. This connectivity enhances the sense of community and can foster a supportive environment for personal growth. However, it also poses challenges, as individuals may grapple with issues of validation, comparison, and self-worth in the digital realm. The interplay between online and offline identities can create tensions that influence personality development in complex ways.

In conclusion, writing is a powerful force in shaping personality. Through various forms of writing—whether journaling, creative expression, academic discourse, or online sharing—individuals engage in a continuous process of self-exploration and reflection. Writing allows us to articulate our thoughts and emotions, fostering self-awareness and emotional regulation. It encourages us to explore different facets of our identity, challenge our beliefs, and assert our voices in a world that often seeks to define us.

As we engage in writing, we not only convey our experiences but also shape our very selves. The act of putting pen to paper—or fingers to keyboard—invites us to delve into the depths of our personalities, guiding us toward greater understanding and authenticity. Through this ongoing dialogue with ourselves, we cultivate resilience, empathy, and a more nuanced sense of identity, ultimately enriching the tapestry of our lives. Writing, therefore, is not just an act of creation; it is an act of becoming.

Writing to Enhance Critical and Clear Thinking: Lessons from Great Minds

The art of writing transcends mere communication; it is a powerful tool for refining our thoughts and enhancing our ability to think critically and clearly. Throughout history, thinkers such as Jordan Peterson, Leonardo da Vinci, Theodore Roosevelt, and Benjamin Franklin have demonstrated how effective writing can shape their ideas, influence their actions, and cultivate a profound understanding of the world. By examining their approaches to writing, we can glean valuable insights into how to enhance our own critical thinking and clarity through the written word.

The Power of Writing in Critical Thinking

Writing is inherently an act of thinking. When we write, we are forced to organize our thoughts, articulate our ideas, and engage in self-reflection. This process demands clarity, coherence, and logical structure—key components of critical thinking. As we put our ideas into words, we examine our assumptions, challenge our beliefs, and refine our arguments.

Jordan Peterson: The Importance of Articulation

Jordan Peterson, a contemporary psychologist and author, emphasizes the significance of articulation in his work. He often discusses the idea that clear thinking is closely tied to clear expression. For Peterson, writing is not just a means of conveying information; it is a method for developing and clarifying thoughts.

One of Peterson's notable practices is his insistence on writing down thoughts and arguments in a structured manner. He suggests that when individuals engage in writing, they must confront their ideas and assess their validity. For example, in his book "12 Rules for Life," Peterson presents complex philosophical and psychological concepts in a clear and accessible way. This clarity is achieved through careful organization and thoughtful articulation of his arguments.

To emulate Peterson's approach, one can start by outlining key ideas before diving into writing. This technique encourages a logical flow of thoughts and helps identify gaps in reasoning. For instance, if writing about a personal experience, one might begin with the main lesson learned, followed by the circumstances surrounding that experience, the emotions involved, and the broader implications. This structure ensures clarity and encourages deeper reflection.

Leonardo da Vinci: The Art of Notetaking

Leonardo da Vinci is often celebrated as a polymath whose curiosity and creativity knew no bounds. His approach to writing was deeply intertwined with his quest for knowledge. Da Vinci kept extensive notebooks filled with observations, sketches, and reflections on various subjects, from anatomy to engineering. His notetaking was not merely a means of recording information; it was an essential part of his intellectual process.

Da Vinci's notebooks illustrate the importance of continuous inquiry and reflection in critical thinking. He wrote not just to document but to explore and understand. His habit of questioning assumptions and seeking connections between different fields is a testament to how writing can enhance clarity and critical thinking.

To adopt da Vinci's method, one might keep a personal notebook dedicated to exploration and inquiry. This could include jotting down questions about everyday experiences, sketches of observations, or reflections on readings. By treating writing as a tool for discovery rather than just a means of communication, individuals can foster a mindset of curiosity and critical analysis.

Theodore Roosevelt: The Value of Discipline in Writing

Theodore Roosevelt, the 26th President of the United States, was not only a charismatic leader but also a prolific writer. He wrote extensively throughout his life, producing works ranging from political essays to autobiographies. Roosevelt believed that discipline in writing was essential for clear thinking and effective communication.

Roosevelt's writing process was characterized by rigor and commitment. He famously set aside time each day for writing, viewing it as an essential part of his routine. His disciplined approach allowed him to articulate complex ideas clearly and persuasively. For example, in his autobiography, Roosevelt reflects on his experiences and values, offering insights into his worldview. The clarity of his writing reflects the discipline he cultivated through consistent practice.

To follow in Roosevelt's footsteps, one could establish a daily writing routine. Setting aside dedicated time each day for writing—whether journaling, drafting essays, or composing letters—can enhance both writing skills and critical thinking. By treating writing as a daily practice, individuals can develop clarity of thought and a stronger command of language.

Benjamin Franklin: Writing as a Tool for Self-Improvement

Benjamin Franklin, one of the Founding Fathers of the United States, exemplified the idea of writing as a means of self-improvement. Throughout his life, Franklin engaged in various writing exercises aimed at refining his character and intellect. His famous "13 Virtues" were documented in his writings as a framework for personal development.

Franklin's approach involved setting specific goals for improvement and documenting his progress. He would reflect on his daily actions and assess whether they aligned with his virtues. This practice not only encouraged self-reflection but also sharpened his critical thinking skills. By writing about his experiences, Franklin gained insights into his behaviour and decision-making processes.

To adopt Franklin's method, one might create a personal development journal focused on specific goals. This could involve writing about virtues one wishes to cultivate, reflecting on daily experiences, and assessing progress over time. By committing to this practice, individuals can enhance their self-awareness and develop a more thoughtful approach to personal growth.

The Art of Clarity in Writing

Clear writing is synonymous with clear thinking. When our writing lacks clarity, it often reflects muddled thoughts. To write clearly, one must engage in critical thinking and self-reflection. The following strategies, inspired by the writing practices of great minds, can enhance clarity in writing:

1. **Outline and Structure**: Before beginning to write, create an outline that organizes key ideas. This helps maintain a logical flow and prevents rambling.
2. **Use Simple Language**: Avoid jargon and overly complex vocabulary. Strive for simplicity, as it fosters understanding and engagement.
3. **Be Concise**: Aim to express ideas succinctly. Eliminate unnecessary words and phrases to enhance clarity and impact.
4. **Revise and Edit**: Writing is a process. Take the time to revise and edit drafts, focusing on clarity and coherence.
5. **Seek Feedback**: Share your writing with others to gain different perspectives. Feedback can illuminate areas that may need clarification.

The Interplay Between Writing and Critical Thinking

Writing is not just a solitary act; it is often a dialogue with oneself and with others. The interplay between writing and critical thinking can be illustrated through the following concepts:

1. **Reflection**: Writing encourages reflection on experiences and ideas. This reflective process leads to deeper understanding and insights.
2. **Questioning**: The act of writing often raises questions that challenge assumptions. Critical thinking thrives on inquiry, prompting individuals to explore different perspectives.
3. **Argumentation**: Writing persuasive arguments cultivates critical thinking skills. Crafting a well-reasoned argument requires analysis, synthesis, and evaluation of evidence.
4. **Synthesis**: Writing encourages the synthesis of ideas from various sources. This process of integration enhances cognitive flexibility and broadens understanding.
5. **Empathy**: Writing about diverse perspectives fosters empathy. Engaging with different voices and experiences cultivates a more nuanced worldview.

The Benefits of Writing for Critical Thinking

Engaging in writing exercises yields numerous benefits for critical thinking. The following points highlight how writing enhances cognitive processes:

1. **Clarity of Thought**: Writing forces individuals to articulate their thoughts, promoting clarity and coherence.
2. **Enhanced Problem-Solving Skills**: Writing about problems and potential solutions encourages analytical thinking and creativity.
3. **Improved Communication Skills**: Clear writing translates into effective communication, allowing individuals to convey their ideas persuasively.
4. **Greater Self-Awareness**: Writing fosters introspection, helping individuals recognize their biases, values, and motivations.
5. **Increased Creativity**: The act of writing encourages creative thinking and exploration of new ideas.

Practical Exercises for Improving Writing and Critical Thinking

To cultivate better writing habits that enhance critical thinking, individuals can engage in specific exercises:

1. **Daily Journaling**: Set aside time each day to write about thoughts, experiences, and reflections. This practice encourages self-awareness and clarity.

2. **Argument Mapping**: Choose a controversial topic and map out arguments for and against it. This exercise enhances analytical thinking and fosters a deeper understanding of complex issues.
3. **Creative Writing Prompts**: Engage in creative writing exercises that encourage imagination and exploration of diverse perspectives.
4. **Book Summaries**: Write summaries of books or articles, focusing on main ideas and arguments. This practice enhances comprehension and synthesis skills.
5. **Peer Review**: Exchange writing with peers and provide constructive feedback. This collaborative process fosters critical thinking and strengthens communication skills.

Incorporating these insights into our writing practices can lead to significant improvements in both personal and professional domains. As we write, we not only communicate but also shape our thoughts, challenge our beliefs, and embark on a journey of intellectual discovery. Writing, therefore, becomes not just a skill but a profound means of engaging with the complexities of life and our place within it.

Part II:

The Literary Renaissance

Its evident that literature is more than just a collection of written works; it is a profound medium that shapes our understanding of ourselves and the world. Through stories, characters, and narratives, literature offers insights into human experience, emotions, and morality, profoundly influencing personality development. This exploration of how literature shapes personality reveals the complex interplay between text and the human psyche, illustrating how stories not only reflect our lives but also transform them.

From the earliest oral traditions to contemporary novels, literature has been a means of communication, a vessel for cultural heritage, and a tool for personal reflection. When we engage with literature, we enter a realm where we can explore different perspectives, grapple with moral dilemmas, and experience the vast spectrum of human emotions. This engagement fosters empathy, self-awareness, and critical thinking—key components in the development of a well-rounded personality.

The characters we encounter in literature serve as mirrors, reflecting aspects of our own personalities and behaviours. Through their triumphs and struggles, we find pieces of ourselves. For example, the hero's journey in epic tales resonates with our aspirations, while the flaws of tragic figures remind us of our vulnerabilities. When we identify with characters, we begin to understand our motivations, desires, and fears more clearly. This process of identification can lead to significant personal growth, as we confront our shortcomings and celebrate our strengths.

Moreover, literature cultivates empathy by allowing us to step into the shoes of others. Reading about diverse experiences—whether from different cultures, historical contexts, or socio-economic backgrounds—broadens our understanding of the human condition. Works like Harper Lee's "To Kill a Mockingbird" or Chimamanda Ngozi Adichie's "Half of a Yellow Sun" invite readers to engage with complex social issues and the intricacies of human relationships. This engagement promotes compassion and understanding, qualities that are essential for developing a well-rounded personality.

The moral lessons embedded within literature further contribute to personality formation. Many literary works grapple with ethical dilemmas, challenging readers to consider their own values and beliefs. For instance, Dostoevsky's "Crime and Punishment" delves into the psyche of a young man struggling with morality, guilt, and redemption. Such narratives prompt readers to reflect on their own moral frameworks and the consequences of their actions. As we navigate these ethical landscapes, we become more attuned to our values, which in turn shapes our personality.

The act of reading itself can be transformative. Engaging with literature requires active participation; it demands concentration, imagination, and critical thinking. This engagement fosters cognitive development, encouraging readers to analyze texts, draw connections, and question assumptions. As we grapple with complex narratives, we sharpen our analytical skills and cultivate a deeper understanding of ourselves and the world. This intellectual growth influences our personality by enhancing our ability to think critically, engage in meaningful discussions, and approach life's challenges with a more nuanced perspective.

Additionally, literature serves as a means of self-exploration. Many readers turn to books during times of personal crisis or transition. In moments of uncertainty, literature can provide comfort and guidance. Characters who navigate challenges similar to our own can offer reassurance that we are not alone in our struggles. This connection fosters resilience, allowing readers to cultivate coping strategies and a sense of agency. Works like "The Alchemist" by Paulo Coelho encourage readers to pursue their dreams, reinforcing the belief in one's capacity for change and growth.

The relationship between literature and personality is also shaped by the social context in which we read. Our interactions with others, including discussions about literature, can enrich our understanding and interpretation of texts. Book clubs, literary discussions, and educational settings provide opportunities to engage with diverse viewpoints, challenging our preconceived notions and broadening our perspectives. These dialogues can lead to profound shifts in how we perceive ourselves and the world, ultimately influencing our personality.

Moreover, the literary canon itself has a significant impact on personality development. The themes, characters, and narratives that dominate our reading experiences shape our values and beliefs. Exposure to diverse voices and genres—such as classic literature, contemporary fiction, poetry, and non-fiction—enriches our understanding of the human experience. This diversity allows us to develop a multifaceted personality that embraces complexity and nuance.

While literature has the power to shape personality, it is important to recognize that this influence is not uniform. Individual experiences, backgrounds, and contexts play a crucial role in how we engage with texts. Factors such as culture, education, and personal circumstances can significantly affect our interpretation of literature and its impact on our personality. This variability underscores the unique relationship each reader has with literature, as it resonates differently depending on one's life experiences.

The transformative power of literature is also reflected in its ability to inspire action. Many individuals are moved by the stories they read, leading to a desire to effect change in their own lives or in society. Literature has the potential to spark social movements and promote awareness of critical issues. For instance, the impact of works like George Orwell's "1984" or Aldous Huxley's "Brave New World" extends beyond their narratives, challenging readers to think critically about power, control, and individual freedom. This inspiration can lead to personal activism, which further shapes an individual's personality as they engage with the world around them.

Literature also facilitates a form of dialogue between the self and the text. This introspective engagement allows readers to explore their beliefs, values, and identities. As we grapple with the themes presented in literature, we often find ourselves questioning our choices and motivations. This self-inquiry fosters personal growth and development, as we learn to align our actions with our values, ultimately shaping our personality.

Additionally, the emotional resonance of literature plays a crucial role in personality formation. Stories evoke feelings—joy, sorrow, anger, and love—allowing readers to experience a range of emotions in a safe and controlled environment. This emotional engagement fosters emotional intelligence, as readers learn to navigate their feelings and understand the emotions of others. The ability to empathize with the experiences of characters deepens our connections with others and enriches our interpersonal relationships.

As we journey through literature, we also encounter universal themes—love, loss, conflict, and redemption—that resonate with the human experience. These themes allow us to reflect on our own lives and the choices we make. By exploring the complexities of human relationships and the struggles faced by characters, we gain insights into our own behavior and motivations. This reflection fosters self-awareness and personal growth, shaping our personalities in meaningful ways.

Furthermore, literature often serves as a form of escapism, offering readers a temporary reprieve from their daily lives. In times of stress or uncertainty, immersing ourselves in a captivating story can provide comfort and solace. This act of escape can be transformative, allowing readers to return to their lives with a renewed sense of purpose and clarity. The insights gained from literary experiences can lead to shifts in perspective and behavior, ultimately influencing personality.

The accessibility of literature in today's digital age has further democratized the transformative power of reading. With the rise of e-books, audiobooks, and online literature platforms, individuals from diverse backgrounds can engage with texts that resonate with them. This accessibility fosters inclusivity, allowing a broader range of voices and experiences to shape our understanding of the world. As we encounter diverse narratives, our personalities become enriched by the multiplicity of human experiences.

As we delve deeper into the intersection of literature and personality, it becomes evident that literature serves as both a mirror and a window. It reflects our inner selves while offering glimpses into the lives of others. This duality is fundamental to the transformative power of literature. By engaging with stories that resonate with our experiences, we gain insights into our motivations and desires. Simultaneously, by exploring narratives that differ from our own, we broaden our understanding of the human experience, fostering empathy and connection.

In conclusion, literature wields a profound influence over personality development. Through its ability to evoke emotions, provoke thought, and inspire action, literature shapes our understanding of ourselves and the world. By engaging with diverse narratives, grappling with moral dilemmas, and cultivating empathy, we foster personal growth and development. As we immerse ourselves in literature, we embark on a journey of self-discovery, ultimately becoming more nuanced individuals. The transformative power of literature lies not only in the stories we read but in the ways those stories resonate within us, shaping our identities and guiding our paths in life. Through this intricate relationship, we find that literature is not just a reflection of our lives; it is a catalyst for change, inviting us to become the authors of our own narratives.

The Impact of Literature on the Human Psyche: A Study of Dostoevsky, Tolstoy, and Dickens

Literature holds a profound power over the human psyche, shaping thoughts, emotions, and behaviours. The works of authors such as Fyodor Dostoevsky, Leo Tolstoy, and Charles Dickens exemplify this influence, presenting complex characters and moral dilemmas that resonate deeply with readers. Through their narratives, these authors illuminate the human condition, exploring themes of love, despair, morality, and redemption. This exploration examines how their writings can impact the human psyche for better or worse, delving into the psychological, emotional, and social dimensions of their literary contributions.

The Human Condition: A Dual Lens

At the heart of the works of Dostoevsky, Tolstoy, and Dickens lies an exploration of the human condition. Their characters grapple with existential questions, ethical dilemmas, and the consequences of their actions. Through this lens, readers gain insights into their own lives, reflecting on their choices, beliefs, and values. The psychological impact of these narratives can be both uplifting and unsettling, depending on the themes and characters portrayed.

Dostoevsky: The Depths of the Human Psyche

Fyodor Dostoevsky's works delve into the complexities of human nature, often exploring themes of suffering, guilt, and redemption. His novels, such as "Crime and Punishment" and "The Brothers Karamazov," present characters who face moral crises, illuminating the darker aspects of the human psyche.

The Positive Impact

1. **Exploration of Guilt and Redemption**: Dostoevsky's characters often confront profound guilt, forcing readers to engage with their own moral frameworks. For instance, in "Crime and Punishment," Raskolnikov's journey from guilt to redemption invites readers to reflect on the nature of morality and the possibility of forgiveness. This exploration can lead to personal growth, as individuals consider the impact of their actions and the potential for change.
2. **Empathy for Suffering**: Dostoevsky's focus on the struggles of his characters fosters empathy

in readers. By portraying the depth of human suffering, he encourages an understanding of the complexities of mental health and moral dilemmas. Readers may come away with a heightened sensitivity to the struggles of others, promoting compassion and understanding in their own lives.
3. **Existential Reflection**: The existential themes present in Dostoevsky's work challenge readers to confront their own beliefs and the nature of existence. This can lead to greater self-awareness and a deeper appreciation for the nuances of life. Engaging with these profound questions can inspire readers to seek meaning and purpose in their own lives.

The Negative Impact

1. **Psychological Distress**: While Dostoevsky's exploration of guilt and suffering can be enlightening, it can also lead to psychological distress. Readers may become overwhelmed by the weight of existential questions or the portrayal of despair. This emotional burden can provoke feelings of hopelessness or anxiety, particularly for those who are already grappling with their own mental health challenges.
2. **Morbid Fascination**: Dostoevsky's focus on the darker aspects of human nature can sometimes lead to a morbid fascination with suffering and depravity. Readers may become

desensitized to violence or moral ambiguity, potentially normalizing unhealthy behaviors or attitudes. This phenomenon can skew perceptions of reality and influence individuals to adopt a more cynical worldview.
3. **Isolation and Alienation**: The intense psychological struggles faced by Dostoevsky's characters can evoke feelings of isolation in readers. The depth of despair and the existential crises depicted may resonate too strongly, leading individuals to feel disconnected from others. This sense of alienation can hinder interpersonal relationships and promote feelings of loneliness.

Tolstoy: The Search for Meaning

Leo Tolstoy's literary contributions, including "War and Peace" and "Anna Karenina," explore themes of love, family, morality, and the search for meaning in life. His narratives are rich with philosophical reflections, providing readers with a broader understanding of existence and human relationships.

The Positive Impact

1. **Moral and Ethical Reflection**: Tolstoy's emphasis on morality invites readers to reflect on their own ethical beliefs and practices. His exploration of the consequences of actions, particularly in "Anna Karenina," encourages

individuals to consider the moral implications of their choices. This introspection can lead to personal growth and a stronger alignment between one's values and actions.
2. **Appreciation for the Ordinary**: Tolstoy's portrayal of everyday life, particularly in "War and Peace," fosters an appreciation for the beauty in simplicity. His characters often find profound meaning in ordinary experiences, encouraging readers to cultivate mindfulness and gratitude in their own lives. This perspective can enhance overall well-being and satisfaction.
3. **Connection to Humanity**: Through his exploration of human relationships, Tolstoy emphasizes the interconnectedness of individuals. His narratives remind readers of the importance of compassion and empathy, fostering a sense of solidarity with others. This connection can inspire altruism and a commitment to social justice.

The Negative Impact

1. **Moral Absolutism**: While Tolstoy's emphasis on morality can be beneficial, it may also lead to a rigid understanding of ethics. Readers might adopt a black-and-white perspective on moral issues, struggling to navigate the complexities of real-life situations. This absolutism can hinder personal growth and adaptability.

2. **Existential Nihilism**: Tolstoy's search for meaning can evoke feelings of despair for some readers, particularly if they struggle to find purpose in their own lives. His exploration of existential questions may lead individuals to confront their own lack of fulfillment, resulting in a sense of nihilism. This can be particularly challenging for those grappling with identity or purpose.
3. **Overwhelming Idealism**: Tolstoy's idealism regarding love, family, and morality can create unrealistic expectations. Readers may feel pressure to embody these ideals, leading to disappointment when faced with the imperfections of life. This dissonance can contribute to feelings of inadequacy and self-doubt.

Dickens: The Power of Social Commentary

Charles Dickens' novels, such as "A Tale of Two Cities" and "Great Expectations," are known for their vivid characters and incisive social commentary. Dickens explores themes of social injustice, class disparity, and the transformative power of love and friendship.

The Positive Impact

1. **Awareness of Social Issues**: Dickens' work serves as a powerful critique of societal injustices, raising awareness of issues such as

poverty and inequality. This social consciousness can inspire readers to engage with their communities and advocate for change. The empathetic portrayal of marginalized characters encourages compassion and a desire for social reform.
2. **Redemption and Transformation**: Dickens frequently explores the theme of redemption, illustrating the potential for personal growth and change. Characters like Ebenezer Scrooge in "A Christmas Carol" exemplify the possibility of transformation through love and kindness. This message resonates with readers, instilling hope and the belief in the capacity for change.
3. **Interpersonal Relationships**: The emphasis on friendship, family, and human connection in Dickens' works highlights the importance of relationships in personal well-being. Readers are reminded of the value of empathy, support, and community, encouraging them to foster meaningful connections in their own lives.

The Negative Impact

1. **Sentimentality and Melodrama**: While Dickens' exploration of redemption and human connection is often uplifting, it can sometimes veer into sentimentality. This melodramatic portrayal may lead readers to overlook the complexities of real-life

relationships and societal issues. Such oversimplification can hinder critical engagement with serious social problems.
2. **Nostalgia and Idealization**: Dickens' romanticized depictions of certain characters and settings may lead to an idealization of the past. Readers might yearn for an unattainable version of reality, resulting in dissatisfaction with their own lives. This nostalgia can prevent individuals from engaging with the present and pursuing meaningful change.
3. **Emotional Overload**: The intensity of Dickens' emotional narratives can overwhelm some readers, especially those sensitive to themes of suffering and injustice. The vivid portrayals of hardship may evoke feelings of despair or helplessness, impacting mental well-being. This emotional overload can detract from the transformative potential of his work.

The Interplay of Literature and the Psyche

The impact of literature on the human psyche is not a simple dichotomy of good or bad; it is a complex interplay of themes, emotions, and personal experiences. Readers' backgrounds, beliefs, and mental states significantly influence their engagement with literary texts.

1. **Personal Resonance**: The way a reader responds to a text often depends on their

personal experiences. For instance, individuals who have faced moral dilemmas may resonate more strongly with Dostoevsky's exploration of guilt, while those grappling with social issues may find solace in Dickens' social commentary. This personal resonance can either enhance the positive effects of literature or exacerbate negative feelings.
2. **Cultural Context**: The cultural context in which a reader engages with literature also shapes their understanding. Different societies may interpret themes of morality, justice, and relationships in varied ways. Readers from collectivist cultures, for example, may respond more profoundly to Tolstoy's emphasis on interconnectedness and community than those from individualistic backgrounds.
3. **Psychological Readiness**: The psychological state of the reader plays a crucial role in how literature impacts the psyche. A person experiencing emotional turmoil may be more susceptible to feelings of despair when reading Dostoevsky, while another individual seeking inspiration might find hope in the same text. This variability underscores the subjective nature of literary engagement.

The Healing Potential of Literature

Despite the potential for negative impact, literature also holds immense healing power. The therapeutic effects of reading have been documented in various studies, highlighting how engagement with literature can improve mental health and emotional well-being.

Bibliotherapy: Healing Through Literature

Bibliotherapy is a therapeutic approach that utilizes literature to promote mental health and emotional well-being. The practice involves recommending specific texts to individuals based on their emotional or psychological needs. The works of Dostoevsky, Tolstoy, and Dickens can serve as powerful tools in this context, as they address universal themes of suffering, redemption, and the human experience.

1. **Empowerment Through Stories**: Engaging with narratives that mirror personal struggles can empower readers. For example, individuals dealing with feelings of isolation may find solace in Dickens' characters who overcome adversity through friendship and community. This connection can instill hope and encourage readers to seek similar connections in their own lives.
2. **Reflection and Catharsis**: Literature provides a safe space for reflection. Readers can process their emotions through the experiences of characters, facilitating catharsis. Dostoevsky's exploration of guilt and redemption allows readers to confront their own moral conflicts, leading to deeper self-understanding and acceptance. This process can be profoundly

healing, as individuals learn to navigate their feelings and experiences.
3. **Fostering Resilience**: The stories of resilience in literature can inspire readers to cultivate their own strength. Tolstoy's characters often exemplify perseverance in the face of adversity, encouraging readers to adopt a similar mindset. By witnessing characters overcome challenges, individuals may feel more capable of facing their own difficulties.

Literature as a Catalyst for Change

The impact of literature extends beyond individual transformation; it can also serve as a catalyst for social change. The works of Dostoevsky, Tolstoy, and Dickens address systemic issues, encouraging readers to engage with social justice and advocate for change.

1. **Awareness and Advocacy**: Dickens' critique of social injustice raises awareness of issues such as poverty and child exploitation. Readers inspired by his narratives may feel compelled to advocate for social change, participating in movements that address inequality and injustice. This engagement can lead to a more informed and compassionate society.

2. **Moral Responsibility**: Tolstoy's emphasis on moral reflection encourages readers to consider their responsibilities to others. By engaging with his work, individuals may feel a stronger sense of duty to contribute positively to their communities. This awareness can foster a culture of altruism and support, ultimately benefiting society as a whole.
3. **Challenging Norms**: Dostoevsky's exploration of existential questions and moral ambiguity invites readers to challenge societal norms. This critical engagement can lead to a re-evaluation of personal beliefs and behaviors, promoting a culture of introspection and growth. By confronting uncomfortable truths, readers can contribute to a more just and equitable world.

Conclusion: The Dual Nature of Literary Impact

The influence of literature on the human psyche is multifaceted, encompassing both positive and negative dimensions. The works of Dostoevsky, Tolstoy, and Dickens exemplify this complexity, offering readers a rich tapestry of themes that resonate deeply with the human experience.

While literature can inspire growth, empathy, and social change, it can also evoke psychological distress, moral absolutism, and feelings of isolation. Ultimately, the impact of literary engagement depends on a multitude of factors, including individual experiences, cultural context, and psychological readiness.

In recognizing the dual nature of literature's impact, we can appreciate its transformative potential while remaining mindful of its complexities. Engaging with literature not only fosters self-awareness and personal growth but also encourages a deeper understanding of the human condition. By navigating the intricate interplay of themes and emotions within these texts, readers can embark on a journey of self-discovery, healing, and social awareness that enriches both their lives and the world around them.

Through the lens of literature, we find not only a reflection of our inner lives but also a pathway to understanding the broader tapestry of human existence, urging us to confront our realities and aspire to a more compassionate future.

Part III:

The Wisdom Mosaic: Piecing Together a Resilient Perspective

In an age defined by rapid change, uncertainty, and information overload, the importance of cultivating a resilient, holistic, and informed worldview cannot be overstated. Such a worldview serves as a compass, guiding individuals through the complexities of modern life while providing a framework for understanding themselves and their place in the world. It empowers us to navigate challenges, embrace diversity, and engage meaningfully with our communities. This exploration will delve into why such a worldview is essential, why it transcends the confines of news and social media, and the necessity of forming personal opinions on broader existential questions.

The Nature of Resilience

Resilience, at its core, is the capacity to recover from difficulties and adapt to change. It is a trait that enables individuals to maintain their mental health and emotional stability in the face of adversity. Developing resilience involves cultivating a mindset that views challenges as opportunities for growth rather than as insurmountable obstacles. This perspective is vital in a world characterized by unpredictability—be it in personal relationships, career paths, or global events.

A resilient worldview encourages individuals to foster an internal locus of control, meaning they believe they have the power to influence their circumstances. This belief is crucial for mental well-being, as it promotes proactive behaviours and problem-solving. When faced with setbacks, resilient individuals are more likely to analyse the situation, learn from their experiences, and adapt their strategies accordingly. They cultivate a sense of agency, which is essential in maintaining motivation and focus in pursuing their goals.

Moreover, resilience is not a static trait; it can be developed and strengthened over time through various practices, such as mindfulness, self-reflection, and building supportive relationships. Engaging in these practices enhances emotional intelligence, which is the ability to understand and manage one's emotions and empathize with others. This emotional awareness is foundational for effective communication and relationship-building, further reinforcing resilience.

Holistic Perspectives

A holistic worldview complements resilience by promoting an understanding of the interconnectedness of all aspects of life. This perspective encourages individuals to see beyond isolated events or issues and to recognize the relationships between personal choices, societal structures, and global phenomena. A holistic worldview encompasses the recognition that our actions have consequences that ripple through various spheres—social, environmental, and economic.

In a holistic framework, individuals learn to appreciate the complexity of life. This complexity often manifests in social issues, such as poverty, inequality, and climate change, which cannot be addressed through simple solutions. A holistic perspective encourages critical thinking and a deeper analysis of the systems at play, fostering empathy and understanding of diverse experiences and viewpoints. This empathy is essential for building inclusive communities and fostering social cohesion.

Furthermore, a holistic worldview nurtures a sense of responsibility. When individuals understand how their choices impact others and the environment, they are more likely to act with consideration and integrity. This sense of responsibility extends beyond personal behavior to include civic engagement and advocacy for systemic change. A holistic perspective empowers individuals to become active participants in their communities, advocating for policies and practices that promote equity and sustainability.

The Limitations of News and Social Media

While news and social media play significant roles in shaping public discourse and disseminating information, they often fall short of providing a comprehensive worldview. The nature of these platforms can lead to fragmented understandings of complex issues. News is often sensationalized, prioritizing attention-grabbing headlines over nuanced analysis. Social media, while facilitating rapid communication, can promote echo chambers, where individuals are exposed primarily to viewpoints that reinforce their own beliefs.

This environment can create a superficial understanding of critical issues. Relying solely on news and social media for information can lead to oversimplification, where complex problems are reduced to catchy soundbites. Without a more in-depth exploration of topics, individuals may struggle to grasp the full implications of their beliefs and actions.

Moreover, the constant influx of information can lead to overwhelm and desensitization. Individuals may find it challenging to process the sheer volume of news, resulting in apathy or disengagement. A resilient and holistic worldview requires critical engagement with information—analyzing sources, questioning biases, and seeking diverse perspectives. This process necessitates stepping beyond the boundaries of social media and news consumption.

The Necessity of Forming Personal Opinions

Having an opinion on one's worldview is not merely an exercise in intellectual debate; it is a fundamental aspect of personal development and agency. Developing a coherent worldview requires individuals to engage in self-reflection and introspection, examining their values, beliefs, and experiences. This process fosters a sense of identity and purpose, providing individuals with clarity about what they stand for and how they wish to engage with the world.

Forming personal opinions also cultivates critical thinking skills. In a landscape saturated with information, the ability to analyse, evaluate, and synthesize diverse viewpoints is invaluable. Individuals must be equipped to navigate conflicting narratives and discern credible information from misinformation. A well-rounded worldview allows individuals to engage thoughtfully in discussions, making informed choices that align with their values.

Additionally, having an opinion fosters a sense of responsibility toward others and the community. When individuals articulate their beliefs and values, they contribute to the collective discourse, advocating for what they perceive as just and right. This engagement can lead to meaningful actions, whether through community service, activism, or simply fostering open dialogues with others. In essence, personal opinions shape the actions we take and the legacy we leave behind.

The Role of Education and Continuous Learning

To cultivate a resilient, holistic, and informed worldview, continuous education and lifelong learning are essential. Education should not be confined to formal schooling; rather, it should encompass diverse experiences, readings, and dialogues that challenge existing beliefs. Exposure to different disciplines, cultures, and philosophies broadens perspectives and fosters intellectual curiosity.

Engaging with literature, philosophy, and the arts can deepen understanding of the human experience. Classic works by authors like Dostoevsky, Tolstoy, and Dickens explore fundamental questions of morality, identity, and social justice, encouraging readers to reflect on their own beliefs and values. Such engagement cultivates empathy and fosters a deeper understanding of the complexities of life.

Moreover, participating in community discussions, workshops, and forums can provide opportunities for collective learning and growth. Engaging with others who hold different viewpoints challenges individuals to reevaluate their beliefs and expand their understanding of the world. This exchange of ideas is crucial for developing a more nuanced and holistic worldview.

The Intersection of Personal and Collective Responsibility

A resilient, holistic, and informed worldview emphasizes the interplay between personal and collective responsibility. While individuals have agency over their beliefs and actions, they also exist within larger social, cultural, and political contexts. Understanding this interconnectedness allows individuals to recognize their role in shaping the world around them.

Collective responsibility is particularly salient in addressing global challenges such as climate change, social inequality, and systemic injustice. These issues require collaborative efforts and a commitment to working toward solutions that benefit the broader community. A holistic worldview encourages individuals to think beyond their immediate concerns and consider the long-term impact of their choices on future generations.

Furthermore, embracing collective responsibility fosters solidarity and cooperation. When individuals understand that their actions contribute to the well-being of others, they are more likely to engage in practices that promote community health and social justice. This sense of interconnectedness is essential for building inclusive societies that prioritize equity and sustainability.

The Path Forward

Cultivating a resilient, holistic, and informed worldview is an ongoing journey. It requires intentionality, self-reflection, and a commitment to continuous learning. By embracing diverse perspectives, engaging with complex issues, and nurturing critical thinking, individuals can develop a worldview that empowers them to navigate life's challenges with confidence and purpose.

In conclusion, the importance of having a resilient, holistic, and informed worldview lies in its capacity to guide individuals through the intricacies of modern life. It fosters resilience in the face of adversity, encourages empathy and responsibility, and enables informed decision-making. While news and social media provide valuable insights, they cannot replace the depth and complexity that a well-rounded worldview offers. By forming personal opinions and engaging critically with the world, individuals contribute to a more just, equitable, and compassionate society. This journey is not only essential for personal growth but also for the collective flourishing of humanity.

The Relationship Between Worldview and Perception

Understanding the relationship between worldview and perception is crucial for comprehending how individuals interpret their experiences and interact with the world around them. A worldview is a comprehensive framework that shapes our understanding of life, existence, and the nature of reality. It encompasses our beliefs, values, and assumptions about the world. Perception, on the other hand, refers to the process through which we interpret sensory information, forming our understanding of our environment. This intricate relationship influences our thoughts, emotions, and actions, ultimately shaping our experiences and interactions.

Defining Worldview

At its core, a worldview is a lens through which we interpret our experiences. It encompasses philosophical beliefs, cultural values, and personal experiences that inform how we understand ourselves and the world. Worldviews can be influenced by a variety of factors, including upbringing, education, religion, and cultural background. They serve as cognitive frameworks that help individuals navigate the complexities of life, providing a sense of meaning and purpose.

A worldview can be expansive, incorporating a variety of perspectives, or it can be narrow, adhering strictly to specific beliefs. Those with a more expansive worldview are often open to new ideas and experiences, whereas those with a narrow worldview may resist change and struggle to adapt to new situations. This flexibility or rigidity significantly influences how individuals perceive and respond to the world around them.

The Nature of Perception

Perception is a multifaceted process involving the interpretation of sensory information. It encompasses not only what we see, hear, and feel but also how we interpret those sensations based on prior knowledge and experiences. Our perceptions are shaped by various factors, including our physiological state, emotional condition, and cognitive biases. In essence, perception is not merely a passive reception of stimuli; it is an active construction of reality informed by our experiences and beliefs.

The process of perception begins with sensory input—information gathered through our senses. This input is then processed by the brain, where it is interpreted and integrated with existing knowledge and beliefs. The result is a subjective understanding of reality that may differ significantly from person to person. For example, two individuals can witness the same event yet perceive it entirely differently based on their prior experiences, emotional states, and worldviews.

Interplay Between Worldview and Perception

The relationship between worldview and perception is deeply intertwined. Our worldview influences how we interpret sensory information, while our perceptions can reinforce or challenge our existing beliefs. This interplay can be understood through several key dimensions:

1. **Cognitive Biases**: Our worldviews shape the cognitive biases we experience. For instance, confirmation bias—the tendency to seek out information that supports our existing beliefs—can lead individuals to perceive information selectively. Someone with a particular political worldview may focus on news that aligns with their views while disregarding information that contradicts them. This selective perception reinforces their worldview and may lead to polarization.
2. **Cultural Context**: Worldviews are often deeply rooted in cultural contexts. Different cultures may prioritize distinct values and beliefs, influencing how individuals perceive the world. For example, collectivist cultures may emphasize community and interdependence, leading individuals to perceive social dynamics differently than those from individualistic cultures, which prioritize personal autonomy. This cultural influence shapes not only individual perceptions but also societal norms and behaviours.

3. **Emotional State**: Our emotional states significantly impact perception, and these states can be influenced by our worldviews. For instance, someone with an optimistic worldview may perceive challenges as opportunities for growth, while someone with a pessimistic worldview may see the same challenges as insurmountable obstacles. This emotional lens colours their perceptions, affecting how they respond to various situations.
4. **Life Experiences**: Personal experiences play a critical role in shaping both worldview and perception. Significant life events, such as trauma or education, can profoundly alter one's worldview, subsequently influencing how one perceives future experiences. For example, someone who has experienced discrimination may develop a worldview that emphasizes social justice, leading them to perceive systemic issues more acutely than those who have not had similar experiences.
5. **Social Influences**: Interpersonal relationships and social environments contribute to the formation of both worldview and perception. Socialisation processes—how we interact with family, peers, and community—can reinforce or challenge existing beliefs. Individuals may adapt their worldviews based on social contexts, which, in turn, affects their perceptions of social dynamics and relationships.

The Dynamic Relationship

The relationship between worldview and perception is not static; it is dynamic and reciprocal. As individuals encounter new information and experiences, their perceptions may evolve, leading to shifts in their worldview. Conversely, a shift in worldview can alter how one perceives new information and experiences.

1. **Evolving Perceptions**: When individuals are exposed to new ideas or experiences that challenge their existing worldview, they may undergo a process of re - evaluation. This re - evaluation can lead to expanded perceptions and a more nuanced understanding of complex issues. For instance, exposure to diverse cultures and perspectives can broaden one's worldview, fostering greater empathy and understanding.
2. **Reinforcement of Beliefs**: On the other hand, individuals may also experience a reinforcement of their existing beliefs when their perceptions align with their worldview. This reinforcement can create a feedback loop where individuals actively seek out information that confirms their beliefs while dismissing information that contradicts them. This phenomenon contributes to polarization and can hinder open-mindedness and critical thinking.

3. **Critical Reflection**: Engaging in critical reflection is essential for navigating the relationship between worldview and perception. By questioning one's assumptions and beliefs, individuals can create space for growth and adaptability. This reflective process encourages individuals to consider alternative perspectives and engage in constructive dialogues, fostering a more inclusive and comprehensive worldview.

The Importance of Awareness

Cultivating awareness of the relationship between worldview and perception is essential for personal growth and effective communication. This awareness allows individuals to recognize the biases and limitations of their perceptions, fostering a more open and adaptable mindset.

1. **Mindfulness**: Practicing mindfulness can enhance awareness of one's perceptions and the underlying worldviews that shape them. By becoming attuned to their thoughts, emotions, and biases, individuals can make more conscious choices about how they engage with the world. Mindfulness encourages individuals to observe their perceptions without judgment, facilitating a deeper understanding of their experiences.
2. **Empathy and Understanding**: Recognizing that others may have different worldviews

and perceptions is vital for fostering empathy and understanding. Engaging in dialogues with individuals from diverse backgrounds can challenge preconceived notions and broaden one's perspective. This exchange of ideas can lead to greater social cohesion and collaboration in addressing complex issues.
3. **Adaptability**: Acknowledging the fluidity of worldview and perception encourages adaptability. In a rapidly changing world, the ability to adjust one's beliefs and perceptions in response to new information is invaluable. Individuals who embrace adaptability are more equipped to navigate challenges, foster innovation, and engage meaningfully with diverse communities.

The Role of Education

Education plays a significant role in shaping both worldview and perception. A well-rounded education encourages critical thinking, promotes exposure to diverse perspectives, and fosters an understanding of the complexities of the world.

1. **Critical Thinking Skills**: Education that emphasizes critical thinking equips individuals to analyze information objectively, evaluate sources, and challenge their assumptions. By honing these skills, individuals can develop a more nuanced worldview that accommodates diverse

perspectives and encourages open-mindedness.
2. **Cultural Literacy**: Exposure to different cultures, histories, and philosophies through education fosters cultural literacy, enhancing individuals' understanding of the complexities of human experience. This literacy enables individuals to engage empathetically with others, recognizing the cultural contexts that shape their worldviews and perceptions.
3. **Encouragement of Dialogue**: Educational environments that prioritize dialogue and collaboration cultivate a sense of community and shared inquiry. Engaging in discussions with peers and educators encourages individuals to explore their beliefs and assumptions, fostering personal growth and expanding their worldview.

The relationship between worldview and perception is intricate and multifaceted. Our worldview shapes how we perceive and interpret our experiences, while our perceptions can reinforce or challenge our existing beliefs. This dynamic interplay influences our thoughts, emotions, and actions, ultimately shaping our interactions with the world.

As individuals grow older, the relationship between perception and worldview undergoes significant transformations. This evolution is influenced by various factors, including cognitive development, emotional maturity, personal experiences, and societal influences. Understanding how these elements interact throughout the lifespan can provide insights into how our perceptions of the world and our overarching worldviews change over time.

In early childhood, perception is predominantly shaped by immediate sensory experiences and interactions with caregivers. Children are naturally curious, absorbing information from their surroundings. Their perceptions are concrete, often tied to tangible experiences. For example, a child who experiences warmth and affection from caregivers may develop a foundational perception of safety and trust in relationships. Conversely, a child exposed to neglect or conflict may form a perception rooted in fear or mistrust. During these formative years, the worldview is heavily influenced by family, culture, and early education. The values instilled during this period lay the groundwork for future perspectives, as children begin to form basic understandings of morality, community, and belonging.

As children transition into adolescence, they enter a phase of exploration and identity formation. Cognitive development reaches new heights, allowing for abstract thinking and critical analysis. This is a time when individuals start to question previously held beliefs and explore diverse perspectives. Adolescents may find themselves influenced by peers, media, and broader societal narratives. This exposure often leads to a re - evaluation of their worldviews, as they confront new ideas and experiences that challenge their upbringing. For instance, a teenager might begin to engage with social issues, leading to an expanded perception of justice and equality. The ability to think critically allows adolescents to recognize the complexity of issues, but it can also lead to confusion and internal conflict as they navigate competing beliefs.

In young adulthood, individuals typically solidify their worldviews as they accumulate experiences and engage with diverse communities. Higher education often plays a pivotal role during this stage, exposing individuals to new ideas, cultures, and philosophies. As they encounter differing perspectives, they may refine or reshape their beliefs. This period is marked by an increased awareness of societal structures, leading many to question established norms. For example, a young adult who volunteers in a community organization may develop a deeper understanding of social inequality, resulting in a more nuanced worldview that prioritizes empathy and social justice.

The transition into middle adulthood often brings about a shift in focus. Individuals frequently reassess their priorities and values, often influenced by career developments, family responsibilities, and life experiences. This stage may prompt individuals to reflect on their past perceptions and consider how those have shaped their current worldview. For many, this is a time of increased emotional maturity, leading to a more integrated perspective that balances personal aspirations with communal responsibilities. As they face life's challenges—such as raising children or caring for aging parents—they may develop a more complex understanding of relationships, resilience, and interconnectedness.

In later adulthood, the relationship between perception and worldview can be characterized by a deeper wisdom that comes from a lifetime of experiences. Older adults often reflect on their lives, integrating lessons learned into a cohesive worldview. This stage may be marked by a sense of acceptance, as individuals come to terms with their experiences and the passage of time. Many find themselves more open to the perspectives of others, recognizing the validity of different life experiences. This openness can lead to a greater sense of empathy and understanding, enriching their perceptions of the world around them.

However, it's important to acknowledge that not everyone experiences these transformations in the same way. Factors such as mental health, trauma, and social context can significantly influence how individuals perceive the world and shape their beliefs. Some may cling to rigid worldviews, resisting change even as their perceptions evolve. Others may embrace continuous growth, allowing their experiences to inform an ever-expanding worldview.

The dynamic interplay between perception and worldview throughout life illustrates a journey of self-discovery and growth. As individuals navigate the complexities of existence, their perceptions are continuously influenced by a multitude of factors. By fostering self-awareness and engaging with diverse perspectives, individuals can cultivate a richer understanding of themselves and their place in the world. This journey emphasizes the importance of adaptability and openness to change, ultimately leading to a more profound and nuanced worldview as one progresses through life.

www.ingramcontent.com/pod-product-compliance
Lightning Source LLC
LaVergne TN
LVHW091623070526
838199LV00044B/908